A Man in Overalls

A Man in Overalls

The Legacy of a Cape Breton Bard

JUDY ROY

Red Hawk

Cover image by Wanda Nicholson

Maps and Nicholson Family Tree by Suzana and Elaina White

ISBN 979-8-9906244-0-5 (paperback)

ISBN 979-8-9906244-2-9 (ebook)

For my mother, Anne Marie Kiritsy,
and my uncle, Father John J. Nicholson

Contents

Preface

My maternal grandparents were important fixtures in my life as a young girl. I was their first-born grandchild, so I received a good deal of their attention. Our family lived across town from them in Worcester, Massachusetts, and visited "the folks" at least one evening every weekend. Competitive card games at the kitchen table began soon after we arrived, punctuated intermittently with peals of laughter and heavy table-thumping and knee-slapping, indicating a winning hand had been displayed. Catchy fiddle music played on the Victrola, especially when my grandfather's brother, Uncle Dan, and his wife, Aunt Annie, visited from Gardner. My siblings and I explored the house during these visits and waited for our grandmother to served the tea with milk and homemade bannock or shortbread cookies. These evenings were our American version of the old Scottish Ceilidh (kay-lee)—a kitchen party.

My mother's father, Patrick Nicholson or Papa to me, was the custodian for Ascension Catholic parish in the Vernon Hill neighborhood of Worcester, and I attended first and second grade at Ascension School. My father dropped me off at my grandparents' house every schoolday, I had lunch with them, and Daddy picked me up in the evening. I would skip along the short path from their house to the little school, and my grandparents doted on me whenever I was with them. We were a close family, but I knew very little about my grandfather's early life beyond the fact that he came to the United States from Sydney, Nova Scotia.

Papa Nicholson retired from the parish in 1970 and died in 1972 at age eighty-four, a couple of months after I finished my first year of college at St. Francis Xavier University in Antigonish, Nova Scotia. His obituary in the *Worcester Telegram and Gazette* gave the pertinent facts of his life. He was born in Nova Scotia, Canada, and worked as "a caretaker for Ascension Church." It listed the names of his parents and his survivors, and the times of his wake and funeral Mass. Many people from Vernon Hill paid their respects to the gentle janitor who cared for their parish. He was beloved.

Memories of my grandfather lay dormant within me for years. I graduated from St. F. X., left Nova Scotia, and eventually settled in North Carolina, where my husband and I raised our own family and welcomed grandchildren over the years. Then one day, out of the blue, I received a gift that sent me back in time to my childhood. It was a CD of Cape Breton fiddle tunes, so much like those my grandfather played whenever we visited his house, but reenergized by a new generation of talented young musicians from Cape Breton Island. This familiar music would bring me back to my roots in Cape Breton, Nova Scotia. I was on a path of discovery, seeking my grandfather's origins and achievements.

The genealogical record yielded information about my grandfather and his family. His baptism was recorded in July 1887, and Canadian census records helped me fill in the branches of his tree—siblings and cousins, aunts and uncles, grandparents and great-grandparents. Places, names, and dates were accessible through online databases. However, it was during a trip to the 2016 Celtic Colours music festival in Cape Breton that I made a remarkable discovery—tape-recorded interviews of my grandfather telling the story of his early life.

Over the next eight years, I listened to those tapes many times until I understood the historical timeline. I discovered that my grandfather was raised in Rear Beaver Cove, just up the hill from Beaver Cove which sits on the shore of the beautiful Bras d'Or Lake. Rear Beaver Cove was once a vibrant community that was settled by Papa's grandparents when they fled the Outer Hebrides of Scotland in 1837. His grandmother lived in his home and taught him to love their Gaelic language, culture, and the folklore she cherished. He never forgot her, and through those audio tapes and his writings, he has passed down to us her lessons.

Today, no one lives in Rear Beaver Cove. It was abandoned by 1921 and has been reclaimed by nature. I've walked our ancestral land in Rear Beaver Cove, guided by my third cousins George and Joe MacLean, grandsons of Patrick's first cousin Catherine Monica Nicholson. They have explored and mapped the area for years and have a deep knowledge of the original settlement where our grandparents were born and raised.

I've discovered my grandfather's involvement in the early Cape Breton labor movement. He organized trade unions, attended national labor conventions, and worked to establish a labor party in Cape Breton. He reported on union activities in labor newspapers using the pen name, "A Man in Overalls," for his own safety. That work eventually forced his emigration from Canada to the United States.

Family lore and artifacts expanded my understanding of the character of my grandfather. My mother's memories and those of her siblings about their childhood in Baldwinville and Worcester, Massachusetts were telling. My uncle, Father John, had saved and safeguarded letters and folk tales that his father had written over the years. When he transferred this treasure trove to me, I realized at once that my grandfather's story needed to be told.

Part One is the story of my grandfather's life, based on his writings and voice recordings. I share my discoveries about this Man in Overalls—the decisions he made throughout his eighty-four years that reveal his character, attitudes, and beliefs. Whenever possible, I quote him directly. At other times, I tap into the storytelling genes that I inherited from him to bring historical facts and events to life. Using the tools of a fiction writer, I imagine scenes based on my understanding of true events as he and others described them. In such scenes, the reconstructed dialogue appears in italics.

Part Two is a collection of folklore tales and poems written by my grandfather.

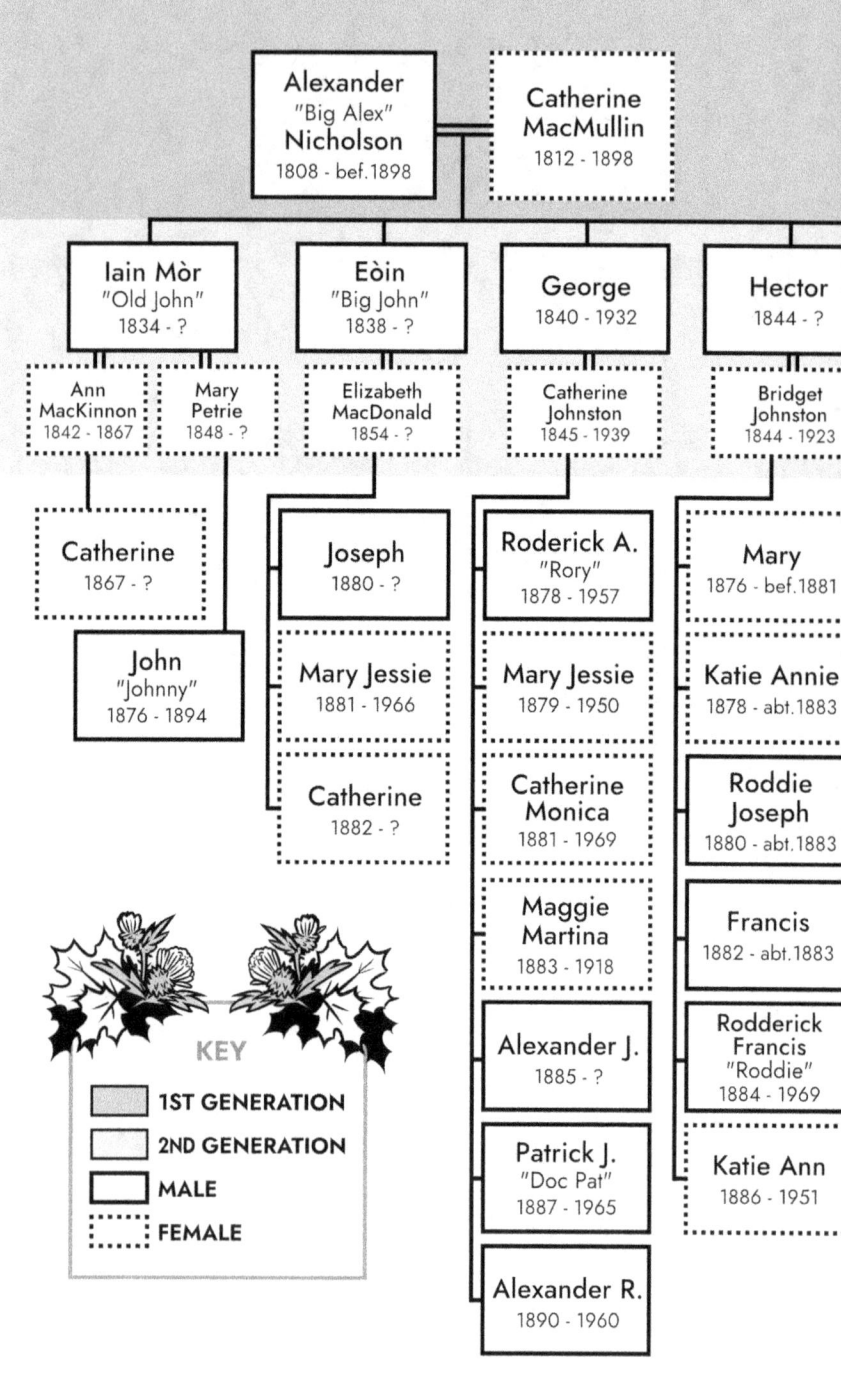

KEY

1ST GENERATION
2ND GENERATION
MALE
FEMALE

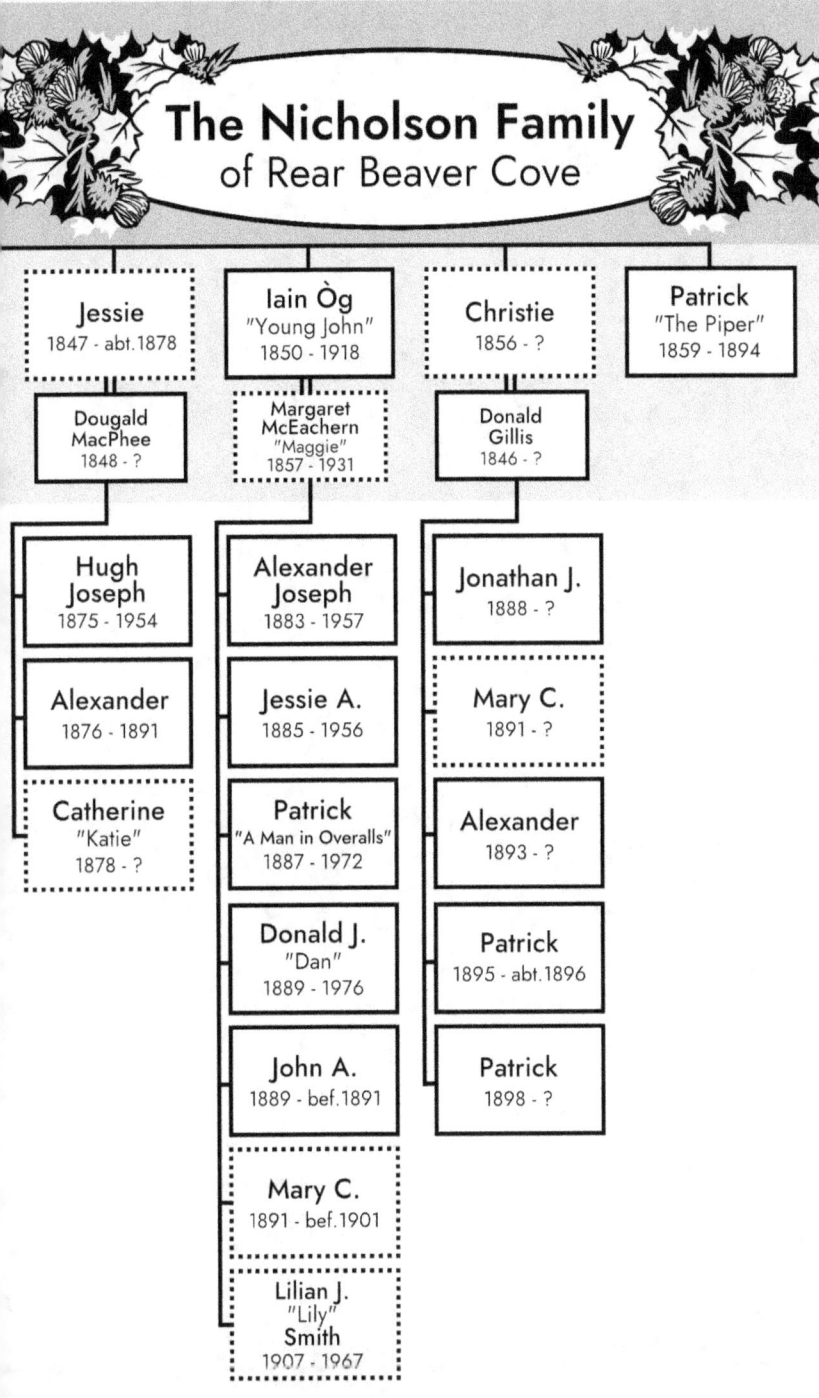

The Nicholson Family
of Rear Beaver Cove

Jessie
1847 - abt.1878

Iain Òg
"Young John"
1850 - 1918

Christie
1856 - ?

Patrick
"The Piper"
1859 - 1894

Dougald MacPhee
1848 - ?

Margaret McEachern
"Maggie"
1857 - 1931

Donald Gillis
1846 - ?

Hugh Joseph
1875 - 1954

Alexander
1876 - 1891

Catherine
"Katie"
1878 - ?

Alexander Joseph
1883 - 1957

Jessie A.
1885 - 1956

Patrick
"A Man in Overalls"
1887 - 1972

Donald J.
"Dan"
1889 - 1976

John A.
1889 - bef.1891

Mary C.
1891 - bef.1901

Lilian J.
"Lily"
Smith
1907 - 1967

Jonathan J.
1888 - ?

Mary C.
1891 - ?

Alexander
1893 - ?

Patrick
1895 - abt.1896

Patrick
1898 - ?

Part One

The Life of A Man in Overalls

Mi coiseachd eadar muir is achadh
Air mór-thìr eile, 's gaoth bhlàth na mara
A'gluasad tarsainn air a' raon, geal le
    seamragan,
'S a' toirt mo sheanar—glan, geur, gràdhaichte—
    gu m' aire.

Walking between field and sea
On another continent, with the warm sea wind
Moving across the plain, white with shamrocks,
Bringing my grandfather—clean, sharp, beloved
    —to my attention.

— Catriona NicÌomhair Parsons,
    "Cuimhne" | "Remembrance"

Chapter 1

A Boy and His Grandmother

I have a cousin in Worcester, Mass. who has a better grasp of family traditions than any other member of the clan. He was a boy of ten or twelve when my grandmother, Catherine MacMillan, died. He lived in the same house with her, was a favorite and imbibed a good deal of her lore.

— Rev. Dr. Patrick J. Nicholson, 1946

They had a special relationship, the young boy and the old woman. It was obvious to everyone in the community. One would rarely see her without him, walking next to her, holding her hand. How unusual for an active child, an energetic boy of eight or nine to show such patience and respect. It was not a chore for him, not something he had to be reminded about; it was instinctive. He loved being with her, his grandmother, and she with him.

Perhaps he knew that her time on earth was growing short. Perhaps he could feel her weakening, leaning ever more heavily upon him during their walks to the garden on pleasant afternoons. He loved this country, this land that was treasured as sacred by everyone who lived there. It was a land that she and his grandfather had settled long before he was born. Little did he know at that time that this community would not go on forever. He couldn't have fathomed that the life of this settlement would one day come to an end.

This is the story of that little boy, who became my grandfather, Patrick Nicholson—Paddy. It begins with his grandmother, Catherine MacMullin Nicholson. She lived with him no more than eleven years, but in that short time, she infused him with her Gaelic spirit and set his life on its interesting course. He once wrote, "I believe that I can say without exaggeration that I knew my grandmother better and lived closer to her during the last ten or so years of her life than anyone else. In fact, she was more of a mother and a teacher to me than anything else. I slept with her, ate with her, learned my prayers from her, and my strong taste for old people and things and a certain idealism and the mystic curiosity that grew in me I owe to her."[1]

The Nicholson home where Paddy lived with his grandmother was in Rear Beaver Cove, Cape Breton, Nova Scotia, Canada. When Catherine and her husband, Alexander, arrived in the area in the late 1830s, it was heavily forested and largely uninhabited, except by the indigenous Mi'kmaq People, who had hunted those woods for thousands of years. Immigrants from Scotland had been arriving in large numbers, seeking land that they could call their own. They established houses, farms, schools, and churches, and their families grew and thrived. By the 1890s, Rear Beaver Cove had become home to three generations, a prosperous settlement of more than forty families.

Like all of the Scottish settlers in Cape Breton, Catherine and Alexander Nicholson brought to the New World their Gaelic language, customs, and folklore as well as their fervent Catholic faith. My grandfather was immersed in this Gaelic culture and attributed his identity to the influence of his grandmother. He wrote, "Granny was a remarkable woman, distinguished in any company. When the old folks would gather, Father MacGillivary would pull over a chair to her side and they would talk and laugh and sometimes she would sing for him. . . . She knew more lovely Gaelic prayers, more songs, stories, and folklore than anyone else I ever knew. Her mind was brilliant, her memory keen, and what old stuff she told me I would not exchange for a thousand volumes; their life in Barra, their courtship and marriage, the immigrants leaving the Isles."[2] No doubt Paddy loved his grandmother very much. He came to believe that he had a right and a solemn responsibility to pass along her wisdom with pride, truth, authority, and honor.

Where did the story of Catherine and Alexander Nicholson originate? Scotland, yes, but what were the particular circumstances that led to their emigration? It was a complex tale, but in the Nicholson household, it was legendary and my grandfather remembered every detail. Paddy knew that they came from the Isle of Barra where his Nicholson ancestors had lived for generations. "They were driven from their homes. They didn't want to leave. They loved their country. But they had to leave. . . . My grandfather, Big Alexander Nicholson, was the first man to settle in the Rears of Beavers Cove. It was in the year 1837."[3]

Chapter 2

The Isle of Barra

*The Catholics live in peace . . . in the islands of Uist and Barra.
. . . Almost all the families are Catholic or disposed to receive
the Catholic Faith if for no other reason, at least to imitate their
ancestors who were so zealous in the cause of religion.*

— Dr. Winster, Prefect of the Scottish missions,
1669

The Outer Hebrides is a chain of islands situated off the northwest coast of Scotland in the North Atlantic Ocean. Many of the fifty constituents are unpopulated, but the Isle of Barra near the southern end of the archipelago has been inhabited for millennia. Barra is a small island, just eight miles in length and four to five miles across. Ocean currents moderate a chilly climate where annual average temperatures vary little, from 44°F (6°C) in winter to 57°F (14°C) in summer. Rainfall is plentiful, especially in the fall and winter months. Summer days are long, but in wintertime, there are no more than seven hours of daylight.

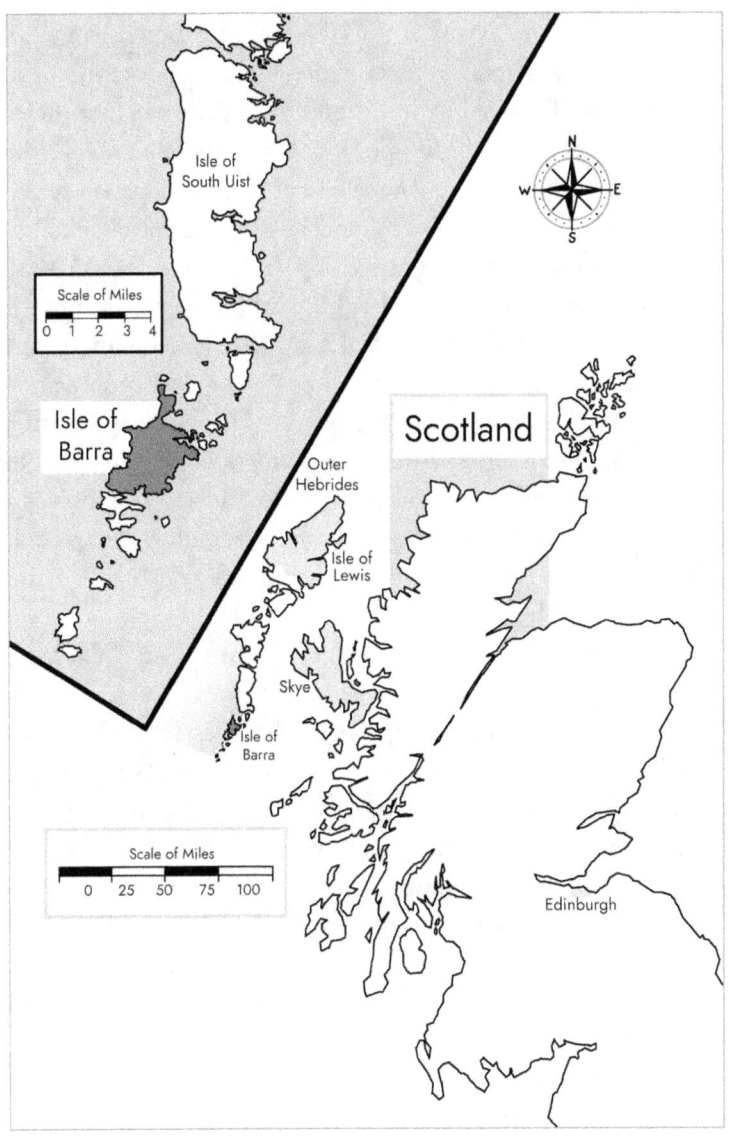

Sparkling white beaches scattered along the west coast of Barra are composed not of sand but an accumulation of "cockle shells . . . ground and pounded into tiny fragments and then compacted to form extensive thick beds."[1] Incessant ocean wind piles the material up into coastal dunes and lofts it into the air so that it settles further inland. There, the calcium-rich particles form the machair, a fertile grassy plain found mainly in the northwestern quadrant of the isle. These grasslands are excellent pasture for cattle, an economically significant commodity for generations of Hebrideans.

The interior of the island is hilly and rock-strewn, unsuitable for home building but ideal for grazing sheep and goats. Below the surface are rich stores of peat, long a valuable source of energy for the local inhabitants. In the time of Catherine MacMullin, islanders spent hours cutting and stacking peat to ensure their homes would always have an adequate supply for the hearth fire. It burned continuously, never allowed to go out. The hearth was the vital source of energy for cooking food and heating their living space.

The landscape of Barra is notably absent of trees. Without a local source of timber, early inhabitants of the island had to rely on driftwood that washed up on the beaches from ships that wrecked while passing through the treacherous surrounding seas. Such precious wood was collected for shipbuilding, roof timbers, and a few home furnishings. People lived in sturdy homes built from the plentiful supply of stones. These primitive stone dwellings proved to be comfortable and warm. Thick walls were made from double layers of unmortared stones stacked several feet high and packed with earth, filling the space between the layers and insulating the home. Traditionally, there was one door and a window or two for light. Timbers, treated with tar, supported a thatched roof, which was made from oat straw tied down with rope and anchored in place with stones to keep the thatch from blowing off in gusty winds. The roof was replaced often and the thatch distributed over the garden to fertilize the soil. These primitive houses had no fireplace nor chimney, but a hole cut in the roof over the cooking fire to let the smoke out. In the eighteenth and nineteenth centuries, this type of dwelling was called a "blackhouse," thought to have been named because the ever-present smoke from the peat fire coated the interiors with black soot.

A reconstructed blackhouse in the village of Arnol on the Isle of Lewis. Photos by author.

Before 1750, the typical diet of Barra's people was based around barley meal, supplemented whenever possible with fish or shellfish, beef or mutton, milk, and cheese. After the potato was introduced in the mid-1750s, it was widely adopted as the dietary mainstay. Potatoes were nutritionally dense, easy to grow, required little cultivation after planting, and had a long shelf life. During the century following the transition to a potato-based diet, the population on the Isle of Barra surged. But when potato blight hit the crop, there was widespread misery for those who had become dependent upon it for sustenance.

Faith

Unlike much of the rest of Scotland, the people of Barra and its neighboring island, South Uist, have remained faithful to their Catholic faith from antiquity. The teachings of the Church were brought to them by missionaries from Ireland who arrived on the west coast of Scotland in the middle of the first millennium. St. Finbar, the bishop of Cork, is thought to have visited Barra in the late 500s; the island may have taken its name from him.[2] Around that time, Colum Cille, later known as St. Columba, was cast off from his native Ireland and landed on the tiny Scottish isle of Iona in the Inner Hebrides. There, he established a thriving monastic community that seeded numerous satellite missions throughout the western Highlands and Islands. The Catholic faith as practiced by these Irish missionaries had found a welcome home in Scotland, where it flourished for about a millennium.

The Protestant Reformation in medieval Europe reached Scotland during the sixteenth century. In 1560, the Scottish Parliament outlawed the practice of the Roman Catholic religion. Catholics who refused to convert to the Scottish national church were persecuted and imprisoned, and their property rights were nullified. They were not allowed to become teachers so as not to impose their beliefs on impressionable children. Over time, a majority of Scots, particularly in English-speaking regions, renounced the Roman church. However, Gaelic-speaking inhabitants of the southern Hebridean islands of Barra and South Uist remained among the minority, stubbornly faithful to the religion of their forefathers and their revered saints, including Finbar, Columba, and Brendan the

Navigator. The first church on Barra was named for Saint Brendan.

One barrier to practicing their faith was the scarcity of clergy to administer the sacraments and instruct them in Church teachings. When an Irish missionary, Father Dermott Duggan, arrived in Barra in 1652, he found adults as old as 80 years who had never received the sacrament of baptism, evidence that the island's Catholics had been "deprived of the Sacraments for at least eighty years," yet faithful still.[3] Without the benefit of local priests, island Catholics often "had to rely on oral tradition and lay baptism and marriage ceremonies to keep their religion alive."[4] In 1681, there were twelve thousand Catholics in the Scottish Highlands and Islands with four priests, three of whom were Irish missionaries. One hundred years later, it was estimated that the number of Catholics in Scotland was twenty thousand, but of those, perhaps only twenty owned any significant amount of land. In their enduring poverty and with the restrictions imposed upon them by law, Scottish Catholics were hard-pressed to give their sons the educational opportunities necessary to prepare for the priest-hood. Yet they persisted in their beliefs and treasured their religion, passing it down with fidelity from one generation to the next throughout the centuries.

Paddy Nicholson's grandmother, Catherine MacMullin, was born in Bruthernish on the Isle of Barra in 1812. She was baptized by Father Angus MacDonald at Saint Brendan's Church. Her parents were Iain (John) and Seònaid (Janet) MacMullin, and she was the firstborn in a large family. A sister named Anna, and brothers Hugh, William, Malcolm, and John were all born before Catherine reached her tenth year; two more brothers came after that.[5] She must have had many responsibilities around the home. There was always a baby that needed to be consoled or a child that needed attention. No doubt, she would have been like a second mother to her young siblings. Like most young girls in those days, Catherine would have had many other household responsibilities. They tended the livestock, milking the cows and making butter and cream. They sheared sheep and processed the wool, carding it and making yarn at the spinning wheel. Catherine would have learned from a young age to knit socks and underwear for the family and weave the yarn into a primitive fabric called home-spun for clothing and outerwear. Women worked in the garden planting potatoes and grains on their little crofts in the spring, harvesting in the fall, and ensuring that the food supply would be adequate for winter. In all of these tasks, Catherine would have been at her mother's side as they worked from sunrise to sunset and beyond. In many of their daily routines, they kept themselves happy and content by singing their charming Gaelic songs.

At the end of each day, as night set in, the family would settle around the hearth, keeping warm while they sang songs, shared stories and gossip, and discussed the news of the village. For the children, the discussions between their elders might teach them lessons about ancient historical events, Highland chiefs, or legendary clan battles. Someone might mention news about one of their neighbors, and at the end of the evening, they would pray together saying the rosary or a litany of the saints.

Over the years, Catherine and her siblings must have pieced together fragments of those fireside stories to fashion a cohesive history of their MacMullin clan. The MacMullins had not always lived on Barra. In 1794, Catherine's grandfather, Eòghann (Evan or Hugh) MacMullin received a seven-year lease for a croft at Askernish on the island of South Uist, the long island just north of Barra.[6] There he produced kelp, but when the lease expired in 1801, he was evicted from the land. So Eòghann moved south to the Isle of Barra where he settled in

Bruthernish around 1801. It was a time when there was work to be had on the Isle of Barra, and laborers were in demand. It was a time when Eòghann MacMullin would have been in his prime.

The Isle of Barra had been the home of Clan MacNeil since 1427 when a charter for the island was granted to Gilleonan MacNeil by the King of the Isles.[7] Over the centuries, Gilleonan's heirs, many of whom were named Roderick, inherited the island. In 1720, the thirty-ninth Roderick MacNeil became chief. Clan society in Barra differed little from what it was throughout the Highlands of Scotland. Members of a clan lived together on their chief's land and shared in the ownership of it. They recognized the authority of their chief and pledged loyalty to him. Clans took great pride in their name and loved their chief as a father and provider. In return, the chief retained power and respect; he provided security and protection to his clansmen. Chiefs throughout the Highlands and Islands commanded a standing army of their clansmen, ready to be called into service as needed whenever rival clans threatened attack.

As families grew over time, clan lands expanded to accommodate the growing population; nearby smaller clans might be enveloped into a stronger neighboring clan by attaching themselves to the chief. Intermarriage between clans dispersed the bloodline of the chief throughout the extended family so that everyone could trace their heritage back to him. A chief's power was measured by the size of his estate: land, resources, and manpower. For the most part, this societal structure remained intact until 1745, the year of the Jacobite Rising. That marked a major turning point in Scottish clan society.

It was in 1745 when Charles Edward Stuart, affectionately called Bonnie Prince Charlie, raised an army of about 6000 troops from many of the Highland clans to restore the Catholic

Stuart monarchy to the British throne. The prince was a popular figure, and the Jacobite cause stirred a passion in the hearts and minds of many a Highland clansman. After several promising battles, the Rising culminated in a showdown between British Redcoats and Jacobites on the battlefield at Culloden Moor in April 1746. The Prince's army was defeated soundly in a bloody confrontation. The Bonnie Prince escaped with his life, traveling in exile through some of the Jacobite-friendly territories of the Hebrides and the Isle of Skye en route to France. The defeat at Culloden ended all hope for a return of the Stuart dynasty.

After Culloden, the British government took their revenge on the rebellious Highlanders with the passage of the Dress Act and the Act of Proscription in 1746.[8] These laws prohibited Highland clansmen from wearing their traditional tartan clothing and possessing weapons. Anyone caught in violation was subject to severe penalties, including fines, imprisonment, or banishment to distant crown colonies. The laws accomplished their stated goals; clan chiefs no longer required a standing army because feuding between clans was outlawed. Land that once belonged to the clan as a whole was now merely overseen by the chief. No longer the benevolent father figure, the chief became a landlord, collecting rent from his tenants through his proxy, the tacksman. Tenants farmed small parcels of land called crofts. As their families grew, crofters found it increasingly difficult to support themselves and pay the rent within the limits of the croft system. Consequently, the landlord's income dropped; many sought alternative ways to make their lands more profitable. For those with estates along the seacoast, a fortuitous rise in the value of seaweed kept them afloat.

Kelp

Hebridean Islanders had long known that their gardens produced much higher yields whenever they worked seaweed into the thin soil. Seaweed was plentiful, growing in abundance along the beaches and coastal coves, clinging to rocks and floating in shallow pools. It was a blessing, there for the taking, helping them feed their families.

Abundance of seaweed along the shore at Castlebay, Barra. Photo by author.

One day, however, they would be forbidden from taking the seaweed to their crofts and using it as a fertilizer. That's when it became their misery because their fertilizer was suddenly much more valuable for another quality it possessed. Their landlord would set them to work converting seaweed into "kelp." For a time, Hebridean kelp was highly prized for its use in the cities of England to make glass and soap.

When seaweed is dried and burned in large stone kilns, it is converted into kelp, a thick, oily product high in alkalinity. Large quantities of kelp are needed in glass and soap-making industries. Before 1803, English manufacturers purchased kelp from continental Europe, but Parliament slapped a duty on imported kelp during the years of the Napoleonic Wars. The price of Scottish kelp, including that from the Western Isles, shot up; Hebridean landlords took notice. They had a ready supply of seaweed. All they needed was the labor to convert seaweed into kelp. For many a Scottish landlord, the tenants on his estate were just that—the labor. With an abundance of seaweed along the rocky coastline of Barra, kelp-making was an industry waiting to be exploited.[9]

Colonel Roderick MacNeil of Barra persuaded many of his tenants they could satisfy their debt to the estate by working in kelp production. During summer months, they toiled in shoulder-deep seawater, cutting seaweed from the rocks, gathering it into rafts and floating them into shore at high tide, raking it from shoreline to higher ground, spreading it out to dry, and then burning it for at least eight hours in kilns. The entire process was "very labour intensive and unhealthy."[10] Many crofters had to abandon their food plots in the summertime, moving their families into temporary dwellings close to the shoreline. Year after year, their crofts were neglected during the critical growing season, resulting in poor harvests. Often, kelp workers and their children suffered malnutrition because they were unable to grow enough food during the summer to sustain themselves for the duration of the winter. They couldn't quit kelp production, because the rent would be due, and kelp was the only way to make enough money to pay the bill.

Landlords like Colonel Roderick MacNeil of Barra realized huge profits; not so did their tenants. At its peak, kelp brought in £22 per ton of which little more than £2 was paid to the workers. Occasionally a tenant tried to abandon the backbreaking work of kelp burning and returned to the croft. In response, the landlord simply cut the size of the croft without cutting the rent for it, thereby "encouraging" his tenants to stay in kelp-making.

Yet inflated prices for Scottish kelp did not last forever. Parliament lifted the duty on Spanish kelp (barilla) when the Napoleonic Wars ended in 1815. Hebridean landlords were faced with the sudden loss of substantial income. Crofters left behind the kelp production and returned to their plots, which had deteriorated over the years. Many found they were unable to sustain themselves and pay their rent. Talk among crofters of emigration to places like America, Canada, or Australia began to take on a new urgency. By 1822, the year that Colonel Roderick MacNeil died, fireside discussions in many Barra blackhouses centered around rumors about a land far beyond the coastline of Barra, a land called New Scotland—Nova Scotia.

A ten-year-old Catherine MacMullin, my great-great-grandmother, might have overheard her father Iain and grandfather Eòghann discuss current events around the hearth in 1822. The conversation might have gone like this, as Eòghann began:

Iain, when we lived on the croft in South Uist, we produced two and a half tons of kelp in 1798. We got just over £1 a ton. It was impossible to work harder and impossible to pay the rent with that amount of income. Still, we can't know what the future holds for us, so let's just trust in God. Remember, we have managed before, and, please God, we will manage again.

That's true, Father. We managed, but look where it has gotten us now! When kelp was valuable, Colonel MacNeil was after making big profits. Then he cut our crofts and raised our rents. Now they can't give away the kelp, the market for it is gone and do you think the rent has been lowered? No, it has not! How are crofters expected to earn enough to feed our own families, never mind the laird and his family, too? I heard it said that just before he died, Colonel MacNeil claimed to be saddened at "the loss of so many decent people . . . much to be regretted."[11] First, the <u>Hector</u> *in 1773 and then the* <u>William Tell</u> *in 1817 took Barramen to Nova Scotia. Now this year,[12] fifty more have gone across the ocean on the* <u>Harmony</u>. *I'm afraid the loss of those decent people is just the beginning. Now that the Colonel is no longer with us, what is our future with his son, General Roderick MacNeil, the new chief? What will he do when there are no crofters left, all gone to take grants of land in Cape Breton? He's inherited his father's debts along with the castle. Will he be wise enough to make up for his father's losses? Only time will tell.*

Had Iain MacMullin and his father, Eòghann, recognized then, in 1822, that they were witnessing the beginnings of a mass exodus of their countrymen to Nova Scotia? If the uncertainty surrounding the transition of landlords, from Colonel Roderick MacNeil to his son, General Roderick MacNeil, gave them hope that things could improve, many others failed to share their optimism. Over the years, large numbers of Catholic Gaels from Barra and South Uist embarked on voyages to one of the growing communities around Loch Bras d'Or in Cape Breton. Time and again, the MacMullins bade farewell to those who couldn't wait. Would there come a time when the MacMullins would decide to abandon their homes in Bruthernish? What would be the final straw for them? Would the decision be their own, or would their landlord force them off their crofts, evicted as Eòghann had been from South Uist many years ago? Would the coming potato and grain crop failures in 1836 push them "to the very edge of starvation?"[13] Perhaps soon all of these factors would play a role.

Chapter 3

Just a Question of Time

Bleak the day they sailed away / Those trusty,
    brave Highland men.
Their homes and crofts in ashes gray / Sepa-
    rated from their kith and kin.
Packed in filthy ships as slaves / Torn from
    customs - native sod,
With no star or chart to guide them / But their
    humble trust in God.

— P. McE. Nicholson, "The Highland
Immigrant"

C atherine drew her cloak close to her, wrapping it securely around the tiny infant sleeping in her arms. She hoped the brisk wind would not awaken him as she stepped through the door of their wee Barra home, but she couldn't fight the urge to get out into the sunshine. It had been a long winter with rain and storms keeping her indoors for weeks on end. Aside from the welcome change of weather, the coming of spring this year signaled other changes that were going to disrupt her life in a very vital way.

She crossed the path in front of the house and started climbing the hill, stopping now and then to catch her breath and survey her surroundings. Behind her at the bottom of the hill lay the small cluster of stone houses where she and her husband lived amongst family and neighbors. Sometimes she still thought of herself as a MacMullin, the eldest daughter of Iain and Seònaid. How dear was her family to her, all the babies and wee ones that she helped raise! Now Rory, her youngest brother, was nearly grown at twelve years old; William would have been nine this year had he not died so young. *Someday perhaps Alexander and I will name a son William*, she thought.

So much had changed over the past year. Now she was a married woman, wed to Alexander Nicholson, Big Alex as he was called. They had a beautiful baby boy, named John after Alexander's father. They already knew that their next son would again be named John after her own father. Then, they'd give them each a nickname. Catherine felt sure they would have more children.

With each step up the rocky incline, she felt her heart beat faster, not just with the exertion of the climb but with ever-heightening anticipation for what was about to transpire. By the time she reached the hilltop, her anxiety had built to panic as she peered westward, past the machair to the brilliant green-blue sea. On days like this when the sun shone brightly and the breeze was gentle, Catherine could not imagine why anyone would choose to leave this beautiful island. Barra was the only home she had ever known, her safe harbor. At other times, storm clouds gathered offshore, the wind blew the tops right off the waves crashing on the beach and rain came down as if from buckets, in every direction at once. Then, it was a wonder any living creature could carve out an existence on such a wild and remote island. The thought of starting a new life in a distant and foreign land made the hair on her arms stand up and a chill run down her back.

Scanning the horizon, Catherine considered how changes on the Isle of Barra had impacted her family and neighbors over the twenty-five years of her life. Sometimes, like fair weather, there was prosperity and peace. More often, like an approaching storm, factors outside their control brought fear and worry, and darkness would envelop their lives. During stormy times, their village of Bruthernish and others like it on the wee Isle of Barra bade farewell to their inhabitants. One by one, families recognized that there was no future for them in their homeland. Now, black clouds were gathering. This approaching storm would spell the end for her MacMullin family. They had persevered through the gales for many years; this year, 1837, was different. The balance between staying and going had finally tipped and their departure was imminent.

Hadn't they known all along that this day would come? Wasn't this exactly what her father had predicted that night by the fire so long ago? Catherine remembered how the tone in his voice frightened her. She was just a child of ten, but old enough to recognize the frustration her father expressed. If they could no longer make money with kelp, and if their crofts could not produce enough to feed them and pay the rent, what else could they do but leave Barra? Many a morning she woke up wondering if today would be the day of *their* eviction. Now, fifteen years hence, the answer was coming into focus.

When *General* Roderick MacNeil inherited Barra from his father *Colonel* Roderick MacNeil in 1822, he "found himself in a very difficult position, with a burgeoning population, unable to feed itself and pay its rents, and with creditors pressing for their money."[1] His attempts to revitalize the economic health of the estate were unsuccessful, and he was eventually forced to declare bankruptcy. By 1827, General MacNeil abandoned his home on the Isle of Barra, leaving the island in the hands of his trustees until a buyer could be found. Many families, including the MacMullins, could not wait until 1840 when that purchase was finalized.[2]

Year after year and with much effort, prayer, and faith, Iain MacMullin's family had gotten by on their croft when many of their neighbors did not. Catherine knew many families whose luck had run out; they were evicted and their only option was to leave Barra. Many had gone to Cape Breton where land was plentiful. People were taking two-hundred-acre grants and starting farms. These people were hungry for land that they could call their own. They would never answer to the whims of a landlord again. Although the land was heavily forested, unlike anything they knew or could even imagine, it presented endless opportunities for those willing to cut down trees and plant crops. The best part of all was that they would live among others who shared their traditions, language, culture, religion, and way of life. Gaels from the Hebrides were creating a new world together in Cape Breton, and their Gaelic communities were flourishing.

Finally, in the year 1837, the family of Iain MacMullin was faced with the notice that they would have to leave their croft. They would set sail on the *Cochran* in June. Life would never be the same for the MacMullin clan. Hearing this news, Catherine realized that her father and grandfather's prediction a decade earlier had come to pass at last.

If their departure had been just a few years earlier, before Catherine's marriage to Alexander Nicholson, before their baby John was born, Catherine would have been preparing to leave Barra along with her parents and her siblings. Now, she was Catherine *Nicholson* and she resigned herself to the fact that soon she would say goodbye to her MacMullin family. Whenever thoughts of the coming separation weighed heavy on her mind, she would think about her strong, handsome husband. Naturally, Catherine would miss her parents, her sister Anna, and all her brothers. Now, though, her place was here with her husband, Big Alex. He was a good man, well-known on the Isle of Barra. "He was a craftsman, a very good craftsman. He was a shipbuilder, a cabinetmaker, a mason, and a blacksmith."[3] He had worked hard to hone these skills. His talents had drawn the attention of General MacNeil, who had come to rely upon Big Alex Nicholson, not only for his abilities but also for his trustworthiness. Alex had been implored to make himself available to the General, so Catherine would have to remain with her husband on Barra when her MacMullins left. Catherine and Big Alex would raise a family here in the same way that they had themselves been raised, in the old way with all the old traditions. Most importantly, Father MacDonald would baptize their children into the Catholic Church, and she would teach them to pray and trust in the faith of their fathers.

Counting down the days with growing dread, Catherine had come to accept that it would be many years before she would lay eyes on her father and mother again. There was even a good possibility that they would never be reunited. The *Cochran* would soon depart the harbor at Tobermory—Mary's Well, as they called it—sailing toward the setting sun across that vast Atlantic Ocean. The journey to Canada would last months, but the immensity of time and distance traveled could never sever the ties binding them together as a clan. Perhaps they would be apart, but she would hold them in her heart until her dying day. For Catherine, family was clan, and clan was everything.

She knew that the journey from Barra to Cape Breton was not without peril on the high seas. Storms, an ever-present worry, could disable a ship mid-ocean sending the passengers and crew to a watery grave. Diseases spread readily under the close conditions of such sailing vessels. The *Harmony* lost twenty percent of its passengers on the voyage between Barra and Sydney. Reports of such losses struck terror in the hearts of those whose departure was imminent as well as those who loved them. Catherine Nicholson hoped that her family would be spared through the intercession of her prayers: *Please God, keep the MacMullins safe on their long journey. And help me find the strength to carry on without them.*

A shrill cry drew Catherine's attention back to the baby in her arms as he wriggled himself loose of his swaddling. Repositioning baby John in her arms as she prepared to descend the hill and return home, she may have sung him a soothing Gaelic lullaby. *It seems impossible that you may never see your grandfather again, wee John. He will miss you so much. I'm sure you would have loved hearing his stories but do not worry, my son. Your father will have stories aplenty to keep you happy. Perhaps, if God wills, someday we will reunite with our MacMullin family in a far-off land.*

Chapter 4

Big Alex Nicholson

They had only two trunks, they got ready at a moment's notice, they only took two trunks of goods with them, without money or anything else. One trunk was full of bedclothes and the other trunk was my grandfather's tools.

— P. McE. Nicholson, 1965

His name was *Alasdair Iain Phàdraig* (Alexander John Patrick) Nicholson, but he was called Big Alex. What was it about him that led to that nickname? Perhaps as a youngster, he was taller or stouter than most other boys his age. Certainly, he was not the oldest of the eight children in his family. Born in 1808, Big Alex was younger than all of them but Roderick, who was two years his junior. But there was something big about him. He had a certain strength of body, mind, and heart. He was highly regarded. So everyone called him Big Alex, and he grew into that designation. My grandfather once wrote, "Big Alexander was hardy and wise in the things he knew."[1]

Big Alex had a heightened awareness of his surroundings

and an innate curiosity about the world around him. He could read the land, the wind, the sea, the weather. He learned how nature shaped the lives of people and their property on a small Hebridean island. He could also read people. He was sensitive to their feelings and emotions. He understood the importance of family, and he was fiercely loyal to his own. Indeed, when he reached his mid-thirties and married his love, Catherine Iain Eòghann MacMullin, he had developed into a man of principle, a man of faith.

Big Alex found that he enjoyed working with his hands, and there was always work for fine craftsmen on the Isle of Barra. From building seaworthy boats for local fishermen to black-smithing, Big Alex was the one to summon. His quality work was renowned, and the landlord, General MacNeil, took note. Capitalizing on the good nature of Big Alex, the General let it be known that Alexander Nicholson's services were indispens-able to him. The General had plenty of work to keep Big Alex busy, and as long as this was the case, Big Alex believed they could count on some degree of financial stability. For now, perhaps the best course would be to remain on Barra even as many others were leaving. For now, they would stay.

Big Alex remembered when his eldest brother, Angus, came home with a surprising announcement: *Mary Neil John MacDonald and I will wed, and then we will leave for Cape Breton. We will get a land grant and start a farm of our own at Mabou.* Angus Nicholson was about thirty years old and Mary MacDonald just nineteen at the time they married on November 16, 1824. Soon after, they left Barra and settled on a farm in Mabou, Cape Breton.

How often did Angus and Mary write letters to his family back in Barra? Perhaps they sent word of their safe arrival and news of the 120-acre grant they secured in Mabou. How would such news from Angus have impacted his younger brother, Big

Alex? Did Big Alex regard Cape Breton as a land of infinite opportunity? He was a craftsman and not a farmer, but perhaps someday it would become necessary to follow in Angus's footsteps. He should not rule out the possibility. General MacNeil could not tie him to Barra indefinitely.

Big Alex Nicholson might have been considering such ideas on a warm June day in the year 1837. He and Catherine were preparing to bid farewell to her family. It was strange to imagine how different everything would be after the MacMullins departed. How would his young wife adapt to the absence not only of her siblings but her parents as well? They would soon find out.

* * *

From a distance, Big Alex and Catherine could just discern three masts of a sailing vessel rising from the mist over the bay. The *Cochran* had arrived as expected, and though it was a marvel to witness, it seemed impossible that this barquentine could accommodate all the passengers waiting to board. Catherine strained to see if her brothers and their families were visible in the crowd.

Is that Father? Catherine wondered. *Yes, and there's Hugh, Malcolm, Roderick, Anna, and Mother. They are all here. They will be leaving soon.*

The hours preceding the departure of a ship like the *Cochran* were hectic ones for the ship's crew. All the necessary food, water, and supplies for the voyage had to be loaded before the passengers embarked. Officials identified each one. Trunks containing the few personal possessions of each family were marked and loaded into the hold. Tearful farewells were exchanged between those going and those staying. Amid this turmoil, Catherine and Big Alex arrived at the landing.

Catherine tried to conceal her sadness, but tears welled up in her eyes. She found her parents among other families who were nervously awaiting the call to board. Catherine thought she was well prepared for this moment, having had plenty of advanced knowledge of her family's emigration plans. Nonetheless, she could never have anticipated the emotional storm that engulfed her as the moment of departure closed in. No longer could she ignore her profound feelings of dread, and she began to sob uncontrollably.

She passed baby John to his grandmother for a moment while she turned to her husband for comfort. Big Alex had played out this scene in his mind many times over the past several weeks. He knew how wrenching this moment would be for his young wife. Their families were firmly entwined, Nicholsons and MacMullins. Could he have anticipated his response as he bent over to console Catherine? Had he planned to whisper something in her ear that would change their lives forever? Planned or spontaneous, the result was unmistakable.

Are you sure, Alexander? Can it be true?

Her face beamed with relief, tears of sorrow morphing into tears of joy. Upon seeing her reaction, Big Alex knew in an instant that this was the right decision—they would accompany the MacMullins on their voyage to Cape Breton. For better or worse, Alexander and Catherine Nicholson would leave Barra on the *Cochran* today.

There was little time to make arrangements for the trip. Big Alex secured their passage. *Be back here before we lift anchor or you'll be left behind,* warned the ship's captain. They hurried home to make final arrangements. Catherine gathered some bed linens and clothing in one trunk; Big Alex stowed his work tools in another. These few items would have to suffice. They must return to the *Cochran* now!

As the crowd began to board the ship, Big Alex was

approached by his sister Margaret and her husband, Donald MacInnis. *Alexander, thank God you and Catherine have decided to go to Cape Breton today,* Margaret said. *I've been worried to death about Rory being on his own, but I know it's going to be best for his future. Could you promise me that you'll watch out for him once you get to Cape Breton?*

Big Alex reassured his sister. *Of course, Margaret. Rory is very special to me.*

Turning to his nephew, Big Alex put an arm around the young man's shoulder. *Let your parents know that you will be traveling with me, Rory. When we get our farmland, yours will be next to ours. We are kin and always will be.*[2]

Chapter 5

Finding Land of Their Own

Build houses and live in them; plant gardens and eat their fruits. Take wives and have sons and daughters; find wives for your sons and give your daughters to husbands, so that they may bear sons and daughters. Increase there; do not decrease. Seek the welfare of the city to which I have exiled you; pray for it to the Lord, for upon its welfare yours depends.

— Jeremiah 29:5-7

W hat joy, what relief washed over every passenger on the *Cochran* the day the ship made landfall in New Scotland—Nova Scotia! It had been nine weeks since anyone had touched solid ground, but their many prayers during those sixty-three days had been answered. Now, they raised their voices in one collective song of thanksgiving, praising the good God who granted their families safe passage. Yet there was no time to gloat over their successful voyage and landing. Now was the time to explore this land and find a spot to clear, to build a home, a farm, and a place to call their own.

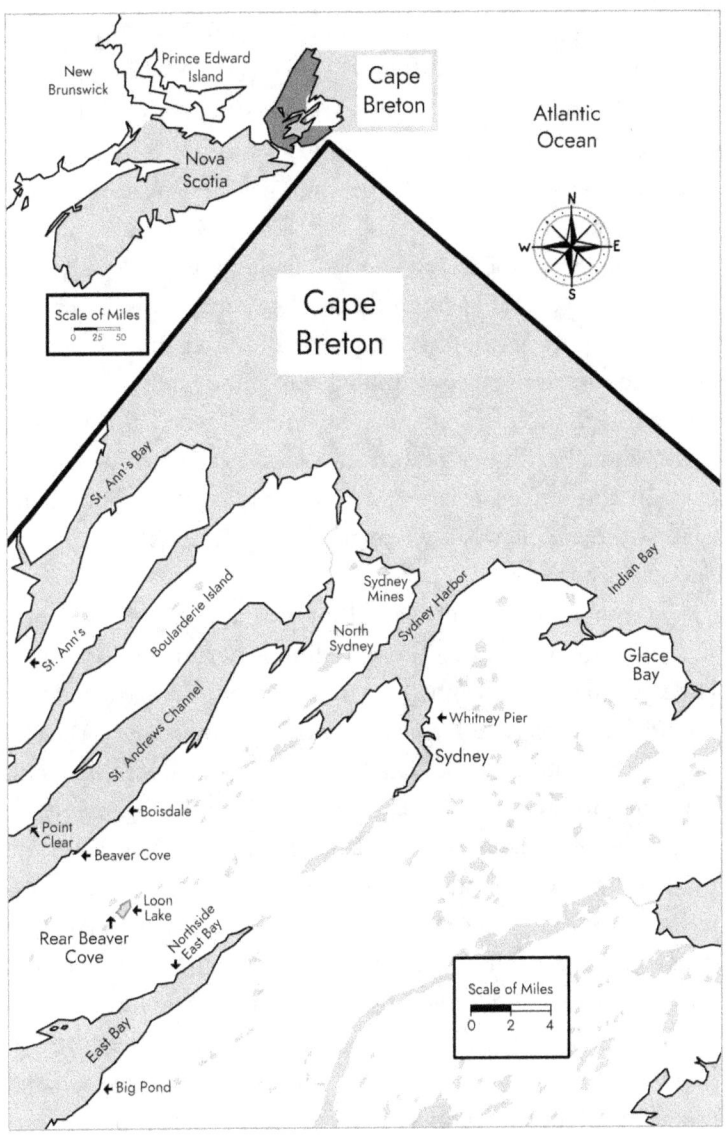

Nova Scotia is made up of two landforms: a peninsula in the west, referred to as the mainland, and, in the east, the island of Cape Breton. The peninsula connects to mainland Canada by a seventeen-mile isthmus at its border with New Brunswick. One of the three Maritime provinces, Nova Scotia is surrounded by the waters of the Atlantic Ocean, the Gulf of St. Lawerence, and the Bay of Fundy. A narrow waterway, the Strait of Canso, separates Cape Breton Island from mainland Nova Scotia. Construction of the Canso Causeway in the 1950s connected the island and mainland parts of Nova Scotia. Countless coves and bays, sandy beaches, rocky cliffs, and headlands line 4600 miles of seacoast. Inland, over three thousand lakes dot a landscape of rolling hills and valleys. Heavily forested in spruce, fir, pine, maple, birch, poplar, oak, hemlock, and tamarack, Mother Nature displays a magnificent coat of color in autumn, especially striking in the northern half of the island—the Highlands—where mountain meets sea along the famous Cabot Trail.

The southern half of Cape Breton is a landscape of gently sloping hills surrounding the sparkling waters of the Bras d'Or Lake. The lake has two basins connected by the Barra Strait at Grand Narrows. The larger southern portion is called the Big Bras d'Or. Little Bras d'Or lies to its north, reaching and stretching toward the northeast, nearly bisected by Boulardarie Island. Several channels and bays, like arms of gold as in the French *Bras d'Or*, embrace the surrounding land. The Bras d'Or is brackish; sea water flows into the lake from the Atlantic through channels along either side of Boulardarie Island and mixes with fresh water entering the lake from several rivers.

The land surrounding the Bras d'Or Lake, not the northern Highlands, attracted Scottish immigrants in the eighteenth and nineteenth centuries. Unlike today's tourists who come to Cape Breton to explore its quaint villages and splendid vistas, these early pioneers were not drawn to the area for its natural beauty or even any particular resemblance to their homeland. For the most part, they came to Cape Breton seeking an escape from oppression at the hands of overlords in the Highlands and Western Islands of Scotland.

European settlers began arriving on the shores of Nova Scotia as early as 1520. The French called their settlement on Cape Breton *Île Royale* in the 1600s but abandoned it in 1659. Gaels from the Highlands of Scotland landed on St. John's Island (now Prince Edward Island) in 1770, and the *Hector* brought Scots to Pictou, on the mainland of Nova Scotia, in 1773. In 1784, a law restricting land ownership in Cape Breton was repealed. Thus began first a trickle, then a torrent, of Gaelic-speaking Scottish immigrants into Cape Breton.

When my ancestors arrived in Nova Scotia, much of the land was still heavily forested, although earlier immigrants had cleared plots along rivers and lakes. Those plots were considered better and more desirable, and they were claimed first. The timber cut from settlements, a valuable commodity, was loaded onto empty immigrant ships and returned to Britain. Later immigrants had to move inland to find enough unclaimed land to start their farms.

Before 1803, there were upwards of ten thousand Scots living in Nova Scotia, a portion of those in Cape Breton. Immigration stalled during the years of the Napoleonic wars, 1803-1815, but thereafter, the Cape Breton population grew with new settlers arriving from the Highlands and Western Isles of Scotland. The population of Cape Breton was 6,000 in 1815. Between 1815 and 1821, about 9,000 immigrants sailed from ports in Scotland to Cape Breton, likely a significant underestimation since accurate records were not kept at the port of Sydney. "There is no means of knowing even roughly the number who landed [in the outports]. . . . Immigrants were set down mostly on the coasts of Cape Breton . . . where the timber ships went, often with passengers for ballast." By 1838, the population of Cape Breton was more than 38,000.[1]

My grandfather was clear in his recollection of the name of the sailing vessel that carried his grandparents from Tobermory to Cape Breton. "They came over on the barquentine named *Cochran*. . . . Well, in the meantime, the better lands were taken along the shore by the first immigrants and the later ones had to take lesser land on the fronts, or less fertile lands in the Backlands."[2] He never mentioned the port of entry, be it Sydney or some other. Maybe he left a hint by revealing, "They came to Boularderie in the year 1837." Perhaps they landed on the island of Boularderie or another outport near it. The harbor at St. Ann's is one possibility. Their berths on the *Cochran* were probably filled up with timber upon their disembarkation.

Imagine the concerns of Catherine and Big Alex when they set out to find someplace to stay in August of 1837. What were their expectations? Did they know people on Boularderie whom they could lean on for a time? Did they simply begin walking away from the ship, looking for available land? The farmland cleared by earlier settlers for crops and grazing was just a fraction of the claimed acreage. Large swaths of forest remained in its virgin state. In the eyes of our ancestors from the windswept, treeless Isle of Barra, what awe, wonder, and even great fear such a view would have inspired. Yet somehow they carried on and spent their first fall and winter on the island of Boularderie with other Gaels from Barra.

Father Patrick J. Nicholson to P. McE. Nicholson,
January 2, 1946. Courtesy of St. F. X. Archives,
RGS/11/12512.

The southern end of Boularderie had been settled by people

from Barra and South Uist who helped fellow Barramen establish themselves in the new country. Autumn was coming fast, so it was too late in the year to plant crops. What would they eat? They would have to rely on others for help with some of their meals, but perhaps they could find other sources of food to sustain themselves during the upcoming winter months.

It seemed wise to choose an island where they could fish the surrounding waters of Loch Bras d'Or. Exploring Boularderie Island, they discovered a stream brimming with fish. *We'll nay starve if we stop here,* Big Alex reasoned. *There's plenty of food swimming in this brook.* So they settled in at Boularderie and weathered their first winter in the new land. Many times, Paddy heard stories about his grandparents' first year and later he wrote about them. "They lived in a hut, hastily constructed of logs with a bark roof, a stone fireplace, no windows, their door a boat sail, their beds made of ground spruce and hemlock boughs and their chairs the two wooden trunks bought at Dunvegan and containing all their earthly possessions. They suffered severely that winter."[3]

It was during this time that Big Alex and Catherine were blessed with the birth of their second son. They named the baby Eòin, Gaelic for Jonathan, but according to the customary practice, he was nicknamed Big John. His older brother, Iain (John), became known as Old John ever after.

Through the kindness of neighbors and the excellent fishing on Boularderie, the young Nicholson family from Barra rejoiced with the coming of spring. They learned many important lessons about survival in their new homeland, not the least of which was the great value of their friends and family. They learned to trust the wisdom of earlier settlers, who shared their knowledge of a wild forested land and how to tame it. They began to understand the unique forces of nature that they faced and the challenges involved in establishing a farm of their own in Cape Breton. It would be a great deal of hard work, but "they weren't afraid of anything or anybody. . . . They worked hard and accomplished whatever they set their mind to."[4]

It soon became clear to them that the majority of good farmland on Boularderie had already been claimed. If they were to have a farm of their own, they would have to pick up and move again. *Boularderie has been a welcome home for us ever since we landed in Cape Breton,* Big Alex might have reasoned. *But we're not going to be able to settle here. There's just not enough good land to sustain our families.*

Beaver Cove lay just across St. Andrew's Channel. Perhaps they had heard that land was available there, or maybe they just decided to explore the possibilities. In any case, they crossed the channel hoping to find the best land that they could. Waving goodbye to the friends who helped them through their first winter, Catherine never forgot their kindness. *May our dear Lord continue to bless you with peace and prosperity,* she prayed.

* * *

After crossing St. Andrew's Channel, Catherine and Big Alex, along with the other MacMullin families and Big Alex's nephew Rory MacInnis, found their opportunity. They passed several settled farms along the Bras d'Or coast in Boisdale and Beaver Cove, the area called the *Frontland* or simply the *Front.* They continued to pass settlements: the second Front, the third Front, and finally one more Front. From there, they climbed up the rugged hillside to the Rear—Rear Beaver Cove.

It was there they discovered acreage plentiful enough to support themselves and their growing families. This is why they left the Isle of Barra! They could settle this land and own it. They would never have to answer to a landlord again. Paddy

Nicholson heard the story many times, describing the details when asked about it seventy years later:

My grandfather [Big Alex] with another boy, his sister's son, who was entrusted to his care, came out to the Backlands and passed three other farms. . . . And they came to a land that they looked over well. . . . They came in the early spring. They looked at the floor of the forest. They looked at the waters, and the rivers, and they considered that this would make them a good home. So they stopped at a spot. And my grandfather, he had an axe, so had [Rory] MacInnis, his nephew, and . . . my grandfather cut a blaze in a tree—a big, very large black spruce tree—and he said, "This will be the line between the two of us."

He asked Rory MacInnis which side of this tree would he want his farm on, and Rory MacInnis said, "I'll take this side, the eastern side."

"All right," my grandfather said [to his nephew], "you walk so many paces in the eastern direction, and I will go similar," and with two axes, they cut down trees in the Backlands . . . which afterward would become a very fine and prosperous place. They built log cabins, and they cleared a spot of ground and they burned the forest of it, and they planted potatoes. That was the beginning of the Backlands.[5]

Chapter 6

The Big Glen

But the early years of their lives in the new world were years of hardship and poverty, of hard labor and constant struggle, of heartache and backache. Hunger was not only their constant fear; the dread of it was a thorn in their flesh, summer and winter.

— P. McE. Nicholson, "The Hill They Blessed"

I can envision my grandfather as a little boy living in a remote cabin in Rear Beaver Cove. He and other family members are sitting around a fire listening to his grandfather tell about the first time he ever set eyes on the farm where Paddy was born. What awe that story must have inspired in a seven-year-old grandson! Would he ever forget that moment? Indeed, my grandfather remembered every detail for the rest of his life. He even gave that land a name, The Big Glen. Many people knew the area by that name.

Without the benefit of official surveys, deeds, or lawyers, the first inhabitants of The Big Glen marked out parcels of land for homes and farms. Their primitive tools—axes, hoes, saws, planes, and adzes—brought the wild country to heel. First, they built homes, not stone-walled blackhouses like the ones they had on the Isle of Barra, but cozy log cabins built from the trees growing on their land. They cleared the forest by axe, one tree at a time, acre by acre. They learned that the virgin soil, exposed after burning the tree stumps, was fertile and produced abundant quantities of potatoes, turnips, oats, and barley. They hunted the woodlands for game and fished the streams. Eventually, they acquired some livestock and cleared more land for pastures. They suffered through long winters with frigid temperatures and snow that accumulated for days on end.

Did these pioneers ever dream about reversing their steps and returning to their homeland in Scotland? Perhaps so, but despite all the challenges, their tight Gaelic community and their prized freedom, including freedom of worship, sustained them. In gratitude to God for all their blessings, the entire community living in the district of Boisdale, including Rear Beaver Cove, contributed the labor and materials to build a church. It opened in 1840.[1] This tiny log chapel was located about six miles from the Nicholson homestead. The parish grew and the church was named St. Andrew's Catholic Church of Boisdale.

Joy and sorrow visited Big Alex and Catherine Nicholson over the years. Their third child was named William after Catherine's brother who died in childhood. Sadly, this infant failed to thrive and perished, despite their efforts to nurture him. They chose a "spot . . . prepared in advance by nature to welcome the body of an angel and there they buried him as there was no ground consecrated by Bishop or priest in the region. But they consecrated it themselves with their faith and simple obedience to God, by their affections for their son, by the sympathy and loyalty of their neighbors, and by the water of their eyes."[2] Soon after, George was born in August 1840; Hector in April 1844.

Big Alex's nephew Rory MacInnis, who had traveled with them to Cape Breton, built his farm next to theirs. Rory married Catherine MacNeil and they started a family of their own. A heavily trodden path between the MacInnis and Nicholson cabins showed how closely the two families relied upon each other. But near tragedy struck the Nicholson household one fateful day in about 1845. They had harvested the grain crop before the barley and oats had ripened. There could be no bread, bannock, or gruel until their quern milled the grains into oatmeal and flour. So they hung sheaves of grain around the warm cabin to hasten the ripening process. Big Alex and Catherine were visiting Rory and Catherine MacInnis next door while the older boys stayed home with baby Hector, asleep in his cradle. Big John, the oldest, "took a brand of fire and he was marching around the house with it," setting some of the hanging sheaves on fire. The fire spread quickly, setting the little log cabin aflame. "By an act of God's mercy," the boys escaped the burning cabin, grabbing the cradle with Hector in it as they fled to safety. The family's first home and everything in it, "the tools and the bedclothes and what was accumulated in the meantime was gone!"[3] But things can be replaced. With help from his kin and neighbors, Big Alex rebuilt that cabin. The Big Glen, along with the family of Catherine and Alexander Nicholson, continued to grow and prosper.

* * *

"The greatest honor you can bestow upon a Scotsman is to name one of your children after him; . . . the Loon Lake country was no exception," my grandfather explained. "There were large families in the 'Big Glen' and naming their children was a matter of great concern. . . . They honored their closest friends in a simple unassuming way with simple unassuming names, and the variety was very small, much less than a dozen male names. 'John' belonged to all clans and sects. . . . 'Donald,' 'Rory,' and 'Neil' were strong names followed by 'Alexander,' 'Peter,' and 'Joseph.'. . . How then were those distinguished, when in a village of say forty families there were at least forty 'Johns' and more because some families had as many as three 'Johns' and their surnames were never mentioned? Yet each name was followed by a characteristic word, either a noun or an adjective, that not only distinguished him from all the rest but also told a great deal about him as an individual unit. We will just state a few of these names: Iain Ban, Iain Due, Iain Daun, Iain Young, Big, Small, Slim; Iain of the Rear, of the Marsh, of the Brook, of the Strait, of the Glen; Iain the Bard, the Blacksmith, the Cooper, the Carpenter, the Shoemaker, the Tailor; Iain the Widow, the Bear, the Ox, and many, many others."[4]

With the birth of each child, Big Alex and Catherine remained true to that Gaelic tradition, naming each in honor of an ancestor. Their first daughter was born in 1847 and named Jessie—Catherine's mother was Jessie (Seònaid) MacKinnon. A second girl, Christie, was born in 1856. Big Alex's mother was Christie (Ciorsdan) MacDougall. The third John of the family, nicknamed Young John (Iain Og), was born in 1850, and the youngest child, Patrick, in 1859. Patrick was a fine piper, the best in the land, but his life was cut short at the age of 24.[5]

* * *

By 1871, Alexander and his sons had cleared and improved forty acres of farmland. The national census conducted that year recorded their agricultural success, enumerating the farm's bounty: eight bushels of barley, one hundred bushels of oats, two hundred bushels of potatoes, and three tons of hay. On thirty acres of pastureland, they raised four milk cows, three other horned cattle, twelve sheep, one horse, and one colt. In the fall, they slaughtered one cow, two sheep, and one pig. Their dairy cows yielded two hundred forty pounds of butter; the sheep gave twenty-four pounds of wool, which was made into twenty yards of cloth. Twenty cords of firewood were cut from their forest. With a home, barn, wagon, and plow, they had become self-sufficient. The Nicholson farm could feed and clothe its growing family. Big Alex and Catherine must have enjoyed a certain sense of pride and prosperity. But they were yet to legally own their farm. Like many of their fellow Scottish immigrants, they were squatting on government property.

The population of Cape Breton swelled with the influx of Gaelic immigrants from the Western Highlands and Islands of Scotland during the first half of the nineteenth century. In 1827, when immigration was at its peak, the government attempted to control the distribution of Crown lands by tightening up regulations. Plots would be sold at auction, requiring ten percent down and the balance within fourteen days. Very few immigrants had the resources to purchase land under such terms. By 1840, "more than half of Cape Breton's population were squatting on Crown land."[6] Many pioneers sought out the poorer land in the Backlands, where they simply found unoccupied property and made it their own.

The Dominion of Canada came into being on July 1, 1867,

when Nova Scotia (including Cape Breton), New Brunswick, Quebec, and Ontario were confederated. Even before that date, as early as 1859, the Department of Crown Lands "was instructed to survey all the occupied holdings on the Island [Cape Breton]."[7] About half of the occupied land was held by squatters, too poor to afford the price of a grant. This situation was less than satisfactory for both the government and the squatters, who could not legally sell or bequeath their farms without owning title to them. In 1872, the price of such land in Cape Breton was set at twenty-five cents per acre, quite a bargain compared to the previous price of forty cents per acre before 1870. After 1872, the price per acre would increase to thirty cents in 1873, thirty-five cents in 1874, and forty cents after that. Many squatters petitioned for grants in 1872 before the discount period ended. However, a worldwide economic downturn after 1872 made it nearly impossible for many of the hopeful rural farmers to acquire the cash necessary to complete the purchase.

Big Alex was keenly aware of talk among his neighbors about changes coming to the district of Rear Beaver Cove regarding the cost of Crown land grants. At the time of the census of 1871, the Nicholson brothers had begun to establish lives of their own. Old John was already a widower at the age of thirty-five and would soon move to Cape North to work at a fish processing company. Big John, age thirty-one, worked as a laborer, not yet married. George, at twenty-nine, had learned the skills of a carpenter, and the younger brothers, Hector and Young John, were farmers. What were their aspirations for obtaining land in Rear Beaver Cove? Perhaps their father conferred with his sons, encouraging them to consider their opportunities at this pivotal time. Would they agree to stake claims on the land the family had farmed for thirty years? In his wisdom, Big Alex might have said something like this: *I hear the*

Crown Land men are coming and our farm will soon be surveyed. It's time we stake our claim on this land. Your mother and I came here from Barra to get land, to farm our own land, and we must do whatever it takes to make this ground legally our own. Without a doubt, they all would agree, knowing that they would have to work harder than ever to accumulate the cash required to purchase their father's 280-acre farm and any additional land they may need.

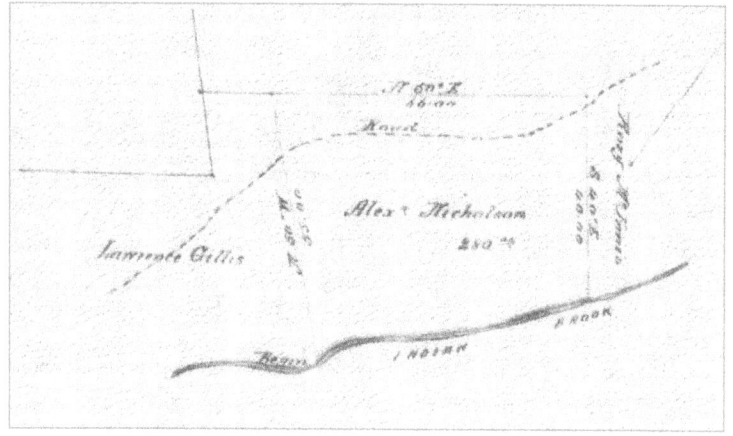

Surveyed boundaries of the Nicholson farm, 1872.

The surveyors came out to The Big Glen as expected, and Big Alex petitioned the government for a Crown Land Grant. His farm was

a Lot of Land, containing two hundred & eighty acres, situated, lying, and being in the County of Cape Breton and bounded as follows: Beginning on the North Western bank of Indian Brook in the district of Beaver Cove, thence coming N 50⁰ by the North Eastern line of Laurence Gillis' land 55 chs [chains] thence N 50⁰ E 66 chs, thence S 40⁰ E by the South

44

Western line of Rory McInnis' land 40 chs to the brook,
thence SouthWesterly by the brook to the place of beginning.[8]

This was the farm that they had occupied and improved, the
farm that sustained their growing family in good years and bad,
from the early 1840s on. To take out the grant, Big Alex was
required to pay the government twenty-five cents per acre, a
total of seventy dollars. He made the first payment of twenty
dollars on April 20, 1872. A second payment of eight dollars
was sent in March 1880. A third and final payment of twelve
dollars was received on February 24, 1882, leaving a balance of
thirty dollars. After ten years, the family had not completed the
purchase of their 280 acres in the Backlands of Beaver Cove.
The farm that they cleared by the sweat of their brows, that they
sowed and reaped every year, and that had always met the family's basic living needs was a farm that could not produce enough
surplus to sell for cash.

The Nicholson family was not alone in this predicament. In
fact, "though many squatters were willing to pay for grants, few
could find the full amount within the allotted time. . . . Very
often balances were never paid. . . . Many had given up the
payments entirely."[9] What a sense of "utter hopelessness." For
so many poor Cape Breton settlers, the dream of owning land
remained just beyond reach. Squatting continued throughout
the nineteenth century, attesting to the "continuing poverty of
much of rural Cape Breton."[10] Eventually, succeeding generations discovered that leaving their homeland was their best
hope, just as it had once been for Big Alex and Catherine
Nicholson, the MacMullin family, and Rory MacInnis in 1837
when they stepped onto the barquentine *Cochran*.

The old black spruce tree that Big Alex blazed with Rory
MacInnis around 1840 had marked the boundary between
MacInnis and Nicholson farms for many years. Then, a govern-

ment surveyor came out to Rear Beaver Cove and showed Rory how his farm was several chains beyond the border he and Big Alex had established when they first set foot on the land. Rory told the surveyor, "No, there's never gonna be a foot of my people go beyond that tree. That's the line, the original line that was made and it's going to remain that way."[11] Hearing this story, my grandfather took the lesson to heart. Rory MacInnis would have been within his rights to use the land beyond the black spruce tree, but he and Big Alex had a covenant that superseded whatever the surveyor determined. When you give your word, you don't take it back. A man is only as good as his word, and Paddy Nicholson became, like his ancestors, a man of his word.

Similar stories of honesty, fidelity, and simple kindness abound in the history of the Gaels of Cape Breton. What was it in the character of these people that fostered such common goodness in the way they lived their lives and interacted with each other? The first generation, the pioneers, established the community with their sweat and tears and modeled those qualities in every aspect of their lives. Their descendants inherited their values and optimism. Is it any wonder they continued the traditions of their ancestors as together they faced new challenges in a new century?

Without knowing where it came from, I witnessed my grandfather's unbounded empathy and kindness during the time that I knew him. There was never a question about his beliefs and sense of duty to his fellow human beings. The more I discovered about the environment in which he was raised, the more I understood how the traditional values of his people laid the foundation on which he structured his attitudes and priorities. This foundation served him well throughout his life.

Chapter 7

Legacy of the Barra Gaels

The present generation can scarcely over-estimate the debt they owe to the early settlers of our country, who not only cleared the land and built comfortable homes but also left a rich tradition of everything that is admirable.

— Rev. Doctor Patrick J. Nicholson, 1926

I t is impossible to know if Big Alex and Catherine Nicholson experienced any remorse or regrets over their failure to secure title to the land they settled in Rear Beaver Cove. We know that they invested what little cash they could scrape together to purchase the grant rights to their farm, but they came up short. Nevertheless, they had escaped a life of servitude, never again to answer to the chief, their landlord. They raised a family of six boys and two girls. They recreated a community of Gaels who spoke their language and shared their beliefs. By the latter part of the nineteenth century, they began to share their land with a new generation of descendants who would be supported, at least in their early years, by the very farm that their grandparents started. This was where my grand-father was born.

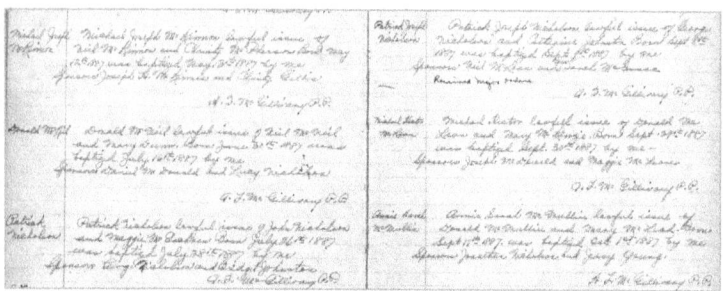

St. Andrew of Boisdale Catholic Church Baptism Register in 1887.
Patrick Nicholson (lower left column) and cousin Patrick J. Nicholson
(upper right column).

Patrick Nicholson met Father MacGillivray when he was just two days old. He was born on the twenty-sixth of July, 1887, and baptized on the twenty-eighth. The priest wrote the pertinent facts into the church register.[1] His parents were Maggie McEachern and John Nicholson. George Nicholson, John's brother, and Bridget Johnston, wife of John's brother Hector, were his godparents. Six weeks later, on September 8, 1887, George's wife Catherine gave birth to a baby boy. This child was named Patrick Joseph Nicholson and he was baptized the very next day. In those times, parents arranged to have their babies baptized as soon after birth as possible. They believed that anyone who died before receiving the sacrament of baptism, even a newborn, could not enter the kingdom of heaven. Instead, the unbaptized would spend eternity in a perpetual state of limbo—neither heaven nor hell. At a time when infant mortality was a real threat, parents breathed a sigh of relief, knowing that, through baptism, their baby's soul would be saved should the unthinkable occur.

Both of these Patrick Nicholsons grew up in the same

community of Rear Beaver Cove, about six miles from the church where they had been baptized. That they were both named Patrick was not particularly unusual in Scottish families, where two or more children within the same household could have had the same first name.[2] It was Gaelic tradition to name a child in honor of an ancestor, thereby carrying forward the memory of that loved one. In this case, it's possible that both Patricks, born just a few weeks apart, were named in memory of their uncle, Patrick *the Piper*. The unmarried brother of George and Young John Nicholson, he died in 1884 at the age of 25. My grandfather said of his uncle Patrick, "As a piper, there was no one that could ever touch him."[3]

Although these young cousins shared the same first name, they were distinguished from each other by their *sloinneadh*, a Gaelic word meaning "patronymic." Thus, my grandfather was *Pádruig 'ic Iain 'ic Alasdair* (Patrick, son of John, son of Alexander). His cousin was *Pádruig 'ic Seòras 'ic Alasdair* (Patrick, son of George, son of Alexander). Last names were not needed, a redundancy.

Whenever children within a family or the community had the same first name, they'd each be called by a descriptive nickname. My great-grandfather was one of three boys named John in his immediate family. He was called Young John; his two older brothers were Old John and Big John, although Big John was actually Jonathan, Eòin in Gaelic. Explaining this practice, my grandfather once said, "Among the Scots, there wasn't more than a dozen names in the whole category of names. There was John in every single family that I know of. . . . Oh, yes, there were nicknames, and their surnames were hardly ever mentioned."[4] My grandfather had a nickname. He was known to his family and friends as Paddy. Later in his life, when he wished to distinguish himself, he used his mother's maiden name as his middle name, Patrick McEachern (P. McE.) Nicholson, signing his stories in that manner. When he felt the need to disguise his identity, he used the pen name A Man in Overalls.

Paddy was the third child of Young John and Maggie McEachern Nicholson. His older brother, Alexander, born in 1882, was named after his grandfather, Big Alex. In 1885, his sister, Jessie, was born and named to honor her aunt Jessie Nicholson, who died in 1878. In 1889, twins Donald and John Augustine were born; only Donald survived childhood. He was named after his maternal grandfather, Donald McEachern, but he was always called Dan. A baby girl born in 1891 died in early childhood. Many children never made it beyond the first few years of life.

Along with my grandfather and his cousin, Patrick, twenty-five other children were baptized by Father MacGillivray in 1887. Donald MacMullin, Alexander MacSween, Agnes Johnston, Mary MacKinnon, and Malcolm MacNeil were some of them. These were the grandchildren of the pioneers who had left their homes in the Western Isles of Scotland before 1840, seeking a better life for themselves and their families. In their quest for that better life, they were successful beyond their wildest imagination.

* * *

I try to imagine life in Rear Beaver Cove during the bustling days of the late 1800s. According to my grandfather, as many as forty families were living in the Rear during his youth.[5] However, the twentieth century brought important changes to Cape Breton, which threatened the sustainability of communities around the Bras d'Or Lake. One by one, the young and the strong abandoned their farms to find work and live their dreams of prosperity in the cities of Cape Breton, western Canada, or in the United States. Many settled in the "Boston States," as it was called. Progress and the promise of better opportunities gradually took a toll on the rural population. By the time the Canadian census was conducted in 1921, not a soul could be found living in Rear Beaver Cove.[6]

Today, a century later, scant evidence remains of the thriving settlement where Paddy Nicholson was born in 1887. Yet those who built the community, especially Paddy's grandparents, left an indelible mark on him. Big Alex Nicholson and his wife, Catherine (MacMullin), lived out the last years of their lives in the home of their son, Young John, his wife Maggie, and their children, Alex, Jessie, Paddy, and Dan. Paddy revered his grandparents, who shared with him the stories of their lives. He learned about how they left their homeland on the Isle of Barra, why they left, and what they endured in leaving Scotland and coming to Cape Breton. They instilled in him a fierce pride for his family, his clan. Indeed, young Paddy understood that, but for a split-second decision in 1837, he might never have seen the light of day, at least not in Cape Breton. He grasped their stories and clung to them because they represented the very foundation of his identity. Later, he found new ways to ensure that his descendants would inherit these stories. Thereafter, it will be up to his children and grandchildren to pass the stories along to future generations.

Chapter 8

Gaelic life and customs

There were three things in every home in the Backlands: a quern, a loom, and a fiddle.

— P. McE. Nicholson, 1965

What would a photographer or an artist have captured of life in Rear Beaver Cove in the late nineteenth century? Is there a scene that would offer us a glimpse into the ways of its people? Although it would be fascinating to discover such a treasure, I'm not sure it would be any more insightful than the recollections of my grandfather, Paddy Nicholson. He told stories of a time and place where everyone pulled together to ensure that the farm would keep families fed and clothed throughout the year. The crops planted in spring, cultivated in summer, and harvested in fall had to be plentiful enough to feed everyone until the next harvest. There were no grocery stores nearby; if they ran short, they did without. Money was of little value to them, except for making payments on the land grant or giving their dues to the church.

They poured every ounce of energy into producing what would be needed for their sustenance.

The Quern

When asked to reflect on his life in Rear Beaver Cove, my grandfather emphasized that every home had three things: a quern, a loom, and a fiddle.

The quern was a primitive device for grinding cereal grains, such as wheat and barley, into flour. In its simplest form, the quern was composed of two circular flat granite stones, one atop the other. Dried grain was poured into the quern through a hole in the center of the upper stone while it rotated against the stationary lower stone. A handle attached to the top stone allowed it to be moved manually. When assembled near a stream, the quern could be driven by the power of running water.

A quern at the renovated Shawbost Norse Mill and Kiln on the Isle of Lewis. Photo by author.

The flour produced by the quern was collected for bread-making. Bannock, a simple unleavened bread made from flour, baking powder, a little sugar, salt, and cream, was quick and easy to prepare. The quern was perhaps the most fundamental implement, for without it, there would be no bread nor porridge, the very staples of their diet. Indeed, the quern was so prized that many immigrants brought the heavy stones with them from Scotland. In Barra as early as the sixteenth century, it was observed that "Every husbandman in the country has one Instrument in their houses called one Kewrne and the two stones doth lye on the house floor, and that place is made clean."[1] Perhaps man cannot live on bread alone, but many can't imagine living without it.

At harvest, Gaels in Cape Breton worked long backbreaking days. This was to ensure that the larder was full before winter set in. Their diet was quite simple, revolving around the few food items that could be produced in quantity and stored for months. Every household dug up many bushels of potato and turnip and reaped large quantities of oats and barley. They cut tons of hay and stored it so they could feed their livestock during the long winter. For protein, they slaughtered a few sheep, cows, and pigs and then salted the meat to preserve it. Fish and shell-fish caught nearby supplemented the diet. My grandfather once said, "We never saw anyone hungry in the Backlands. If you didn't put in a hundred pounds of potatoes, you weren't worth a damn. And if you didn't kill a pig and a steer in the fall and salt it down, you were no good. . . . But that was a general law, there should be a hundred pounds of potatoes, turnips, and cabbage, and that's pretty much what went into it, turnip and cabbage . . . fish and meat, and, God knows, all kinds of bannock."[2]

What happened in bad years when extreme weather or disease destroyed their crops? Perhaps one of the most extreme examples comes from the story of a family left to make due on their own after the untimely death of their father. Neil A. MacKinnon was just four years old when his father died in 1901, leaving his wife with seven young children under the age of thirteen.[3] The family lived on a farm in Rear Beaver Cove, not far from where my grandfather lived at the time. "It was a disaster when you lost your father," Neil said many years later in an interview for *Cape Breton's Magazine.* He remembered the crisis they faced during the winter of 1905, the winter of "the big snow." To make ends meet, his mother had taken on extra cattle, selling butter and milk in the summer. But she didn't "provide for the extra feed for the cattle, and then we'd run out of feed in the middle of winter." For three weeks, the snow came down, blowing in drifts, tapering off before starting up anew, building up to twelve feet in places. The roads in the Backlands were impassable, and people were stranded in their homes. Neil MacKinnon remembered a Nicholson neighbor, who had sold off his cattle because the family was soon moving out of the Rear. This Nicholson offered Mrs. MacKinnon a barnful of hay. Two of Neil's older brothers set off for the Nicholson farm one afternoon at two o'clock, trudging through the deep snow. They hauled out as much as they could in two "bags each slung over their shoulders . . . stuffed with as much hay as you could get in them." They arrived home twelve hours later in the wee hours of the morning. Yet, after all that, the hay that they lugged through the snow "didn't last long." So they organized a *frolic,* where a group of about eight men came together, some of them in snowshoes, to drag about 600 pounds of hay in a light sleigh from the Nicholson farm to MacKinnon's. That got them through until the road from Rear Beaver Cove to Beaver Cove in the Front opened, and they were able to secure a ton of hay from North Sydney arriving by rail car. "That's how we survived during the winter," Neil recalled.

Frolics were a Gaelic custom that thrived in Cape Breton for generations, part of the culture brought over from Scotland by the immigrants. Merriam-Webster dictionary defines frolic as "an occasion or scene of fun; a playful or mischievous action." As practiced in Rear Beaver Cove, frolics bound the community together, neighbors helping each other to get their work done. The milling frolic is a great example of how this custom lightened the load for women during some of their more tedious tasks.

The Loom

It was women's work to produce clothing for the family, starting with shearing the sheep. The fleece was washed and carded by brushing it, like combing tangled hair, to straighten the fibers in preparation for the spinning wheel. That made long strands of yarn. Little girls learn to spin wool using a small hand-held drop spindle. The yarns were woven into coarse fabric at the loom, a necessity in every home. Looms took up a lot of floor space, so they were typically kept in a loft on the upper floor, away from the hustle and bustle of everyday life. The homespun fabric was soaked in gallons of stale urine, which drew out oils and impurities. Nothing worked better. At this point, the cloth was quite rough and coarse, qualities less than desirable for clothing. To improve the texture, it was put through a process called milling or fulling (or waulking in Scotland), which shrunk the fabric and rendered it more waterproof.

When all the homespun had been produced, it was time for the women of the community to come together for a milling frolic. Participants sat across from each other on the long sides of a table with yards of cloth laid out before them. They'd gather up the section of cloth in front of them and begin pounding it on the table in rhythmic synchronicity, slapping it down, sliding it across the wooden boards, toward and away from themselves, then passing their section to the lady next to them to their left. The fabric moved inch by inch around the table. The circular motion was always to the left, clockwise around, because it was considered unlucky to move the fabric in a counterclockwise direction. Gradually over several hours, the gaps between the threads filled in as the fibers relaxed, becoming soft, supple, and water-resistant.

This is where music entered into the story. The rhythms of their movements set the beat for the "milling" or "waulking" song, which began when the lead singer, unaccompanied, started a chorus and the first of many verses, in Gaelic, known by heart from years of repetition. Some of the songs were brought to Cape Breton by the Scottish immigrants; others were written by local poets, known as *bards*. All of the participants joined in on the chorus, sung between each verse. The songs conveyed stories about life, love, and the thoughts and concerns shared by these women. It was considered bad luck to repeat a song during one frolic, which could go on for hours, so the singers had to know a trove of waulking songs.

There were frolics for all kinds of farm and household chores, especially the more tedious ones. The gaiety of the frolic turned a dreaded task into fun while neighbors helped each other accomplish some of their most difficult or demanding chores. Since frolics often required some preparation, they gave folks something to look forward to.

Once the cellars were filled with the harvest bounty and the various repair jobs were completed at the end of autumn, it was time to hunker down and wait for winter to have its way with the district. Plunging temperatures caused most of the Bras d'Or Lake to freeze solid, creating a venue for sports like ice skating, hockey, and horse racing on the glassy surface. Snow was plentiful, but it usually didn't prevent families from getting out to visit each other. Indeed, winter was the ideal time to visit.

The Gaelic word *ceilidh* (pronounced kay-lee) means visit, but in this culture, the ceilidh is more than just a visit. Ceilidh is a celebration of Gaelic culture and kinship, embodying the traditions that everyone treasured, traditions that they pass down from one generation to the next. Ceilidh is music and story, folklore, food and hospitality, and even a little work. The ceilidh custom came to Cape Breton with the Scottish immigrants, and it is one practice that has endured and grown in popularity over the years. Today's ceilidh isn't much like the ones that my grandfather experienced during his youth in Rear Beaver Cove. Often they are held in parish halls and community centers all over Cape Breton. The modern ceilidh, or kitchen party, will probably have hired musical entertainment, such as a Gaelic singer or a fiddler accompanied by a guitar or piano. Such ceilidhs are advertised on posters in shops and restaurants around the island during the summer tourist season, giving locals the chance to share their talents, in an intimate setting, with visitors from all over. At the end of the concert, audience members push their chairs up against the walls to make room for dancing in what are called Cape Breton square sets. These ceilidh dances are easy to learn and a great way to stretch the legs at the end of a long day. Everyone goes home with a huge smile on their face.

The Fiddle

The third item found in every home in the Backlands was the fiddle, the instrument that brought so much joy and gaiety to Gaels in Cape Breton and their ancestors in Scotland before them. Fiddle music, similar to what I had heard on visits to my grandparent's home, was at the heart of social gatherings all over

Cape Breton and certainly in Rear Beaver Cove when Paddy Nicholson was a boy at the end of the nineteenth century. Fiddle tunes were the centerpiece of the ceilidh then and remain so today.

In Paddy Nicholson's time, there was more to a ceilidh than music and dancing. It was common practice to share poetry, storytelling, and conversations about family genealogy and ancestry. Children learned their place in the family as they sat around the fire, listening to the old folks talk about the past. The details must have been repeated over and over, which meant that they would never be forgotten. Without a doubt, Paddy Nicholson received his training in Gaelic folklore and learned his patronymic over many winter eves at the fireside in the Nicholson log cabin.

This is how I imagine a ceilidh in my grandfather's home in Rear Beaver Cove. The year is about 1892. A family assembles in the living room and they begin to prepare their home for an evening of festivities. A blazing fire in the hearth casts a golden glow over the room. The children push the furniture, meager as it is, up against the walls. They know nothing can be left out on the floor in the center of the room. Plenty of open space will be needed.

Snow has been falling all day, collecting in drifts along the cabin walls and windowpanes, obscuring the view from indoors. There's an eerie quiet while nature sleeps under the thick crystalline blanket. Dark, cold, and still, this is a typical winter night in Cape Breton. But the paths leading to this cabin will not be silent for long. Weather won't dampen the excitement nor reduce the turnout. Poor weather only ratchets up anticipation and enthusiasm for fun. The first knock signals that the time has come. Neighbors and kin pile through the door, stomp the snow from their boots, and discard their heavy coats. It's Saturday, it's winter, so it's the night for ceilidh.

Only Scottish Gaelic is heard in this cabin tonight. The stories are spoken and the songs are sung in Gaelic. The evening begins with a song or two. More people arrive, some carrying fiddles. Ladies and girls have balls of yarn and knitting needles so they can work on sweaters or stockings. The room is packed. Musicians begin tuning their instruments before breaking into a lively jig or reel. Young girls and old men take turns step-dancing while everyone else taps their feet to the familiar rhythms. Fiddlers wink at each other whenever they play a transition that provokes a spontaneous *whoop* throughout the crowd. After what must be hours of music and dance, laughter and backslapping, the fiddlers beg for a rest. Refreshments come out —biscuits and bannock, tea and perhaps a wee dram—and the volume drops as everyone catches their breath. Only then, a little voice calls out from the corner:

A Sheanair, Grandfather, would you tell us that story again? The one about Rory Breac.

The voice is that of a young boy, no more than five or six years of age. He is Patrick (Pàdruig Iain) or Paddy, as they call him. He is mature, but not big for his age. He seems taller than other youngsters because of his lanky frame. He seems older than his years because of his confidence. His eyes and hair are brown. He has a prominent nose, a typical "Nicholson nose," people say with a little chuckle. He has a quick wit and a ready smile that brightens up his face. He is smart. Curious. Generous. Kind and thoughtful. Most of all, he is proud of his family and he loves family folklore.

The story he wants Grandfather to tell is well-known in these parts. Paddy remembers every small detail. Though he has heard the tale many times, he never tires of listening to his Grandfather tell it. Something magical happens when Grandfather begins speaking. The characters become real because they are real. Or rather, they were real. Grandfather knows this story because it's one that his grandfather told him as a boy. Grandfather's grandfather's grandfather told the story to his children and grandchildren in Scotland. So the story is true, and it must be remembered. Someday, many years from now, Paddy will tell it to his grandchildren. Does he already realize, even at this young age, that he, of all his family members, will be the one entrusted to remember and pass on the lessons of this story? How will he preserve it for future generations?

The room grows quiet, and everyone turns their attention to the old man sitting close to the hearth. He is Alexander Nicholson, Big Alex as he is known. Until this moment, he'd said little, his silence concealing the pride and satisfaction that swells within him whenever his kinsmen gather in his home. Years of hard work, first in Scotland on the Isle of Barra and then here in Canada, building a farm in Cape Breton and a large family, have taken a toll on his body. Big Alex has lived through most of the century. Likely his time is coming to its natural end. Most of his children are themselves married with children of their own. Many of them are here tonight. They gather around him, sitting on the floor at his feet. The children love ceilidh story time, so it is to them that Grandfather speaks. He clears his throat to begin, drawing everyone a little closer, a little quieter:

Many centuries ago, Viking pirates sailed their boats along the coastline of Scotland looking for suitable landing sites, where they raided homes and farms for livestock and grain. Landing on the Isle of Skye, they were met by a hostile army of Scots. In the battle, some of the invaders were killed, others wounded and left behind when the raiders sailed away. Nichol was one of the wounded. He was taken in and nursed back to health by a local family.

A Man in Overalls

Nichol settled in Skye, learned the Gaelic, married a Skye woman, and raised a family. His descendants were called MacNichol, or Nicholson, and the Nicholson family grew into a formidable Clan. They accumulated large holdings of land, a clan tartan, crest, and a chief holding the Castle Dunvegan.

During the sixteenth century, the reigning Nicholson chief had one daughter but no male heir to inherit the lands and property of the Nicholson clan. So he arranged with the chief of the MacLeod clan that his daughter, Lady Nicholson, would marry the MacLeod chief's son, Torquil MacLeod. At the time of Chief Nicholson's death, all of the Nicholson and MacLeod lands would amalgamate into one, yet each clan would retain its own identity, one as Clan MacLeod, the other as Clan Nicholson.

Big Alex pauses his storytelling. A part of him wishes the music would start up again and leave him rest. It is not to be. Instead, he says,

Paddy, would you ask your mother to bring me a cup of tea. The smoke seems to be bothering me tonight and my voice is getting very hoarse.

After taking a couple of sips, Grandfather continues:

Chief Torquil MacLeod and Lady Nicholson had a daughter, who was called Lady MacLeod. Remember that she was a Nicholson on her mother's side. Lady MacLeod married Chief Rory MacNeil of Barra, the first of the seven Rorys. Rory MacNeil brought his bride from Skye to the MacNeil ancestral lands on the Isle of Barra, and she brought along a train of gentlemen- and ladies-in-waiting as servants. Among them was Rory Breac Nicholson.

Rory Breac married Jessie MacLean of Barra and converted to the Catholic faith. They raised a family in Barra and passed down their faith from one generation of Nicholson to the next until this very day. It will be up to you to continue this tradition with your words and actions. Now, Paddy, can you name all of the descendants of Rory Breac and Jessie Nicholson? Where do you belong in this family?

Paddy knows his patronymic and answers his grandfather without delay: Donald Dun whose son was George, whose son was John, whose son was Patrick the Piper, whose son was John, whose son was you, Grandfather, whose sons are Old John, Jonathan, George, Hector, Patrick the Piper and Young John, whose sons are Alexander, Daniel and PATRICK. That's me.[4]

A hearty round of applause prompts the fiddlers to tune up for the second half of the night's merriment. Dissonant notes merge into perfect harmony, a sure sign that musicians and dancers are ready. They won't stop again until dawn. But for one tired old gentleman, this ceilidh is over. With some effort, Big Alex raises himself from his chair and bids his kinsmen a good night. Before drifting off to sleep, the old man murmurs a fervent prayer of thanksgiving for the gift of Paddy, his precious grandson.

Almighty God, I beg you to watch over Paddy and keep him safe in your loving arms. Our family history has been entrusted to him.

Chapter 9

The Supernatural

There were people who could cure a toothache, a sty, a sprain— people who could see coming events like weddings and funerals beforehand and called it "second sight."

— P. McE. Nicholson, "The Heavy Load"

Supernatural or mysterious occurrences often infused the stories and songs of Cape Breton ceilidh gatherings. These were not typical ghost stories, meant to frighten the audience. Rather, storytellers recounted or sang of their own remarkable experiences, unexplainable by rational observers but observed nonetheless. My grandfather once stated that his grandfather, Big Alex "was not the first nor the last to be guided on sea and land by some supernatural sign unaccountable for by mortals."[1] For many of the Barra immigrants who settled Cape Breton, there was no doubt that some people possessed remarkable powers, such as *second sight* or the ability to heal. Forerunners could be read as warnings of future troubles. Accepting the veracity of these signs and powers did not require superstition, but belief in a good God who interacted with his people in ways that only the faithful could understand. Experience taught the descendants of these immigrants that they had inherited the ability to recognize the power of faith in their lives and communities.

"If you didn't believe in the ghosts that were in the Rear, you were out, you were really out!"[2] In other words, everyone believed in certain supernatural happenings. One of the most common observances was a phenomenon that they called *Jack the Lantern*, or as translated from the Gaelic, the *Pointed Fire*. Many people claimed to have seen it, but its source was unknown. It appeared at night as a flame, like candlelight that seemed to hover above ground, casting no light around or below itself as would a normal fire. The light would grow taller, up to eighteen inches, then shorter, lengthening and shortening. It was believed this light foreshadowed a tragic occurrence or a death. One night it was observed on the shoreline of the lake at Beaver Cove. The next morning, a big black boat arrived at the exact location where the flame had been seen. Lifted out of the boat was a casket holding the body of a woman who was to be buried in the local graveyard. This and other reports like it convinced people that Jack the Lantern was a harbinger of trouble.

How often did miraculous or supernatural events occur in Rear Beaver Cove? I have to think that it was a rare occurrence when someone was cured of a disease, particularly at the turn of the twentieth century in a locale where medical care was virtually nonexistent. People said, "If blood poisoning happens, don't call the doctor—call the priest!" So the parish priest of St. Andrew's Church in Boisdale was a busy man during times of sickness in the district.

Father Alexander F. MacGillivray served his parishioners at St. Andrew's of Boisdale for more than twenty years. Arriving in 1880, he baptized their children, anointed their sick, heard their confessions, administered communion to them during the Masses he offered, and blessed the work of their hands. He spoke their Gaelic language and knew their families like his own. The pioneers who settled the area around St. Andrew's Church and their descendants desired nothing more than raising Roman Catholic priests like Father MacGillivray from within their ranks. This goal could only be reached once they were able to educate their sons in preparation for advanced study at university and the seminary.

Father MacGillivray was not from the Boisdale district, but the county of Antigonish. Located on the Nova Scotian mainland about thirty miles from Cape Breton, Antigonish became the home of St. Francis Xavier University (St. F. X.) in 1855. Father MacGillivray was born in 1847, the son of Angus MacGillivray and Mary MacDonald.As a boy, Alexander MacGillivray attended school in his local district of Antigonish. He took a course of study in the classics, including Latin, theology, philosophy, history, mathematics, and English, so he was well prepared to further his education in preparation for the priesthood. He studied at St. F. X. and was ordained after graduating from the seminary in Quebec in 1873. He was the fifth pastor of St. Andrew's parish and died there in 1903. He is buried in the churchyard cemetery.[3]

As well-educated as he was, Father MacGillivray's schooling in true faith continued long after he left the seminary, during the years that he ministered to the saintly people who resided in the Boisdale parish. These were people who, like Big Alex and Catherine Nicholson, struggled through the hardships of life-threatening diseases, natural disasters, and backbreaking work. Their faith was forged over the years, every day, "like gold tested in fire" (1 Peter 1: 7). Time and again, the faith came out stronger. They inspired their children and grandchildren with the stories of their lives, passing along the deep faith that allowed them to endure the struggles.

Father MacGillivray learned firsthand that faith could work miracles, a lesson that might have been the crowning achievement of his priestly ministry. It happened on a cold winter's eve, when, again, he was called to the community of Rear Beaver Cove. This time, it was a young woman, Mary Gillis, who was lying on death's door. Her husband Archie was the son of Lawrence Gillis, and they lived on the property adjoining the western boundary of Big Alex Nicholson's farm. The year was about 1900. Archie Larry and Mary had a family of six children. Little Neil was just an infant when his mother fell ill with a high fever. Archie Larry sent for the priest and Father MacGillivray arrived, dressed for the blistering cold in his big fur coat and hat. The sick woman lay unresponsive, unconscious. Father MacGillivray went to her bedside, off the kitchen. He took out his book and read some prayers, then anointed Mrs. Gillis. She never responded to his presence.

Someone made the tea for Father, and afterward, he began to leave, putting on his fur coat and hat. He attempted to console poor Archie Larry with words he had probably found to be comforting to many people under similar conditions over the years: *Sure it was the will of God, we don't know why, maybe God wanted her, it was a mystery,* and so forth.

Archie Larry let the pastor finish before he responded, unflinchingly, "No, you're not going like that. I didn't send for you for that sermon. I want you to CURE my wife. And you can do it. But if you haven't got the faith to do it, I have it. I know you can do it, and God will understand my faith. And if God wants a soul, I'm willing to go this minute. But how are my children going to get along without their mother? You can cure that woman and you're gonna cure her before you leave this house."[4]

Many years later, my grandfather recollected this exchange

between Father MacGillivray and Archie Larry Gillis. Whenever the priest was summoned, neighbors and family members showed up to offer support and prayers. Had Paddy witnessed this scene at the Gillis home as a young boy, there to pray with others for the recovery of his neighbor, or had he heard about it after the fact? In either case, Paddy remembered the miraculous outcome. He recalled, "Father MacGillivray got kind of mad and peeved. And he took off his coat and he got another book and he went over to where Archie Larry Gillis's wife was, and he read over her, and he read sincerely, and he was dead earnest, and she turned around and smiled. 'Will somebody give me a drink?' she said."

Mary Gillis was about forty years old when she fell deathly ill and was cured by her husband's faith. She lived to have a few more children, and with her husband, Archie Larry, she raised a family of nine in The Big Glen.

Paddy Nicholson told this story in 1965 to a group gathered in Sydney to record their recollections of life in Rear Beaver Cove. He may have thought that someday, someone listening to this recording might question his testimony. Talk of miraculous cures was hogwash to many people. Faith in modern times was not what it used to be. But to Paddy, there was no doubt. He *knew* that Archie Larry Gillis's wife, a mother of six children, was cured by Father MacGillivray in Rear Beaver Cove. He punctuated the story with these words, "This is no bull, this is truth, this is faith, the faith that was there. And anybody that don't believe it, it doesn't matter to me. It happened! Wasn't that worth hearing?"

* * *

Not long after the death of Big Alex Nicholson, his wife Catherine began to show signs of weakness. She was living with her son, Young John, his wife, Maggie (McEachern), and their children Alexander, Jessie, Paddy, and Dan, presumably in the log cabin that Big Alex had built from the virgin forest so many years ago. Her daughter-in-law, Maggie, was kind and attentive to Catherine, who loved having her grandchildren around her. Grandmother was a loving presence in the home and a natural-born teacher. She taught the little ones their prayers in Gaelic, and she was always ready to break into song or captivate them all with folklore stories from the old country. Maggie and Young John felt honored to have Grandmother living with them in her final years on earth.

Waking well before sunrise, Catherine had come to treasure the quiet and darkness in the house before Young John came into the kitchen to stoke the fire in the hearth. Often it was a dream that awakened her, always a lovely dream about something that happened long ago. Perhaps this was God, reminding her that her time on earth was coming to an end. That would explain these dreams. She had been given more time on this earth than most, more than her parents and her grandparents, more than many of her other family and friends. Indeed, God had blessed her beyond measure.

Catherine allowed her mind to wander back through time. She recalled the fireside in her childhood, sitting with her grandfather in the little stone house, their blackhouse. In one of her recent dreams, it was the day her parents declared that they would have to abandon their croft in Barra and sail to Cape Breton as so many others had done before them. Most vividly, she remembered the moment Alexander agreed to join the MacMullins, boarding the *Cochran* with the hope of starting a farm on land they might own someday, never again to have a landlord over them. Their voyage, the first winter in Boularderie, the birth of their second son, Jonathan, now called Big John; all of these memories came to her in the wee hours of morning before anyone else in the house was stirring.

Just thinking about Big John brought a smile to her lips. When was it? Maybe 20 years ago, when he came back to the Rear with a package he had gotten in the city. *Tea,* he said. *Everyone in Sydney loves tea.* He gave the package to his sister, Christie, and told her to prepare it in boiling water. So Christie took the three-legged pot filled with water, boiled the water over the fire, and added the full pound of tea. Everyone in the house was so anxious to try this new drink, so popular in the fine homes of the city. Perhaps it would replace their favorite beverage, *brochan,* made with boiling water and oatmeal. Christie couldn't wait; she dipped a spoon into the pot and tasted the hot tea. Everyone laughed when poor Christie spit out the first sip, declaring that the concoction was too bitter and strong for anyone to drink. She took the whole pot of tea out the door and dumped it on the ground. *If that's what they're having in Sydney, I'll never be going there myself!* she declared. Everyone but Big John thought it was quite funny. Soon, a spot of tea, as my grandfather always called it, prepared properly and sipped from a cup with a drop of milk, became the most popular drink in Cape Breton.

The dream that awakened Catherine this morning was so surprising. In her dream, she was riding a horse, a big black horse. This horse was Murdy, of course, and she and Murdy were coming up the hill to the Backlands, to Rear Beaver Cove. She rode up to the cabin and looked in the window. There were so many people inside, and one by one, she recognized all of the Nicholsons. It was a ceilidh, and her husband, Big Alex, was playing the fiddle. Rory MacInnis, Alexander's nephew who traveled with them from Barra to Cape Breton, was there, too. And the grandchildren, so many grandchildren now, were all in that cabin. Catherine did not want to wake up from that dream this morning.

Grandmother. *Seanmhair*. That was the name she had grown to cherish. Spoken in Gaelic by her many grandchildren, she felt such pride in the family that she and Big Alex started. Lying in bed with the sun casting the first rays of morning light into her little room, Catherine quietly uttered her morning prayers in thanksgiving to God for her family.

Lately, it seemed that, like herself, the Gaelic was not long for this world. And with the coming of English into the schools and the homes, perhaps the beautiful Gaelic traditions would be lost, thrown out, and forgotten. Would her granddaughters learn to shear the sheep and card the wool? Would they have milling frolics, where they would tell stories and sing to the rhythm of their movements? Would the little ones roll the threads onto spools so their mothers and grandmothers could weave the homespun on the loom upstairs? Would they continue to make their clothes, or would they buy fine goods in the shops and markets?

Would her grandsons learn to trap game for a hearty, meaty meal? Would they help their fathers mend fences, and plant and harvest potatoes, turnips, and oats? Would they learn to make flour by grinding grain with the quern? Would they learn to play the fiddle or the bagpipes, dance, and sing old Gaelic songs? Or would they leave the Backlands and country life for good to work for money in Sydney or the Boston States?

Changes were coming for the Nicholson family. Catherine could sense it. Just like the tea coming into the Backlands, new ideas and opportunities were carried back here from the cities. Perhaps some will stay and farm the land. But for others, maybe for most, it will not be enough. Old John left many years ago to work at the fish plant in Cape North, working for money. Big John moved away to Sydney Mines, earning a living as a coal miner. George learned the carpenter trade in the States. He's been talking about taking the family away from the Backlands, to North Sydney. George knew that he could earn a good living building homes for other people, for money, in North Sydney. If I live to see another day, maybe Murdy and I will ride up here and find no one at all. I hope that dream doesn't wake me tomorrow.

Young John's wife, Maggie, quietly closed the door of the cabin behind her as she stepped out into the morning air. Up the hill she walked briskly, in search of her husband, whom she found mending a fence in the high pasture. Something was not right, and she was trying not to panic.

John, Grandmother cannot be well 'cause she didn't get up. I thought you might want to check on her, Maggie said.

John frowned as he laid his spade on the ground and wiped his hands on his shirt. He had been dreading this day. He followed Maggie down the hill to the cabin where he grew up and where he now lived with Maggie, his children, and his mother.

Tentatively, Young John entered the kitchen and tiptoed slowly down the short hall to the little bedroom where his mother slept. The door creaked as he nudged it open, his eyes drawn to the bed where Mother lay still. He walked to her side and, leaning over the old woman, gently touched her shoulder. What relief he felt when she responded!

Are you not feeling well, Mother? John asked in a soft voice. *Maggie worried about you for not getting up at your usual time this morning.*

There's nothing wrong with me, John, but I'm tired. Don't be worried about me. I'll be up a little later.

But her son was worried as he left her bedside. Coming back into the kitchen, he whispered to his wife, Maggie,

I think we should get Hector over here. He will know what to do.

One of the children was sent to the farm where Hector lived with his wife, Bridget, and their two children, Roddie Francis and Katie Ann. Without delay, Hector arrived at his brother's home and together they decided that it wouldn't be any harm to get the priest. Their mother had reached an advanced age. Her whole life had been one of hard work. She had raised a family of eight children and had buried three of them. She had known the pain of leaving her homeland in Barra and the challenge of starting anew, not once or twice, but three times. She had helped to build a home and a community. When she died, she would pass along to her heirs the treasures that she had accumulated in her life: her abiding faith in God and her love for her Gaelic Scottish culture and tradition. Perhaps it was time for her to receive the last sacraments of her beloved Catholic Church.

As word spread, all of Catherine's children came quickly to be present with their dear mother during her final hours. George and his wife Catherine, with their eldest son Rory George, arrived next, and it was twenty-year-old Rory George who was sent to St. Andrew's Church in Boisdale. Father MacGilivary came out in the early afternoon. He greeted Catherine at her bedside with warm friendship. They spoke quietly for a time, sang songs, and told a few stories. After a while, he closed the door to the bedroom, heard her confession, and anointed her with the last rites of the Catholic Church. When he came back into the kitchen, they gave him a cup of tea and then he went back in the bedroom to say goodbye to the old woman. "If you go before me, be sure to have a place there for me," Father MacGillivray told her. He had tears in his eyes when he returned to the kitchen, and he lamented, "I wish to God my soul was in the condition of the soul of that woman."

As things often were in the country, neighbors began to learn that the priest had come. Soon people started arriving. By evening, the small cabin was full of neighbors in addition to all of the Nicholson and MacMullins. The Gillises and the O'Handleys and the MacInnises and the MacPhees were all there. Someone started telling stories, and the folks were just thrilled listening to the stories.

At about ten o'clock in the evening, Maggie went in to see Catherine and asked her would she take a cup of tea. "Yes, I'll take a mouthful," Catherine replied, "and give them all a cup of tea and see would they go. Maybe they'll go on home so you can get to bed."

So the tea was made and passed around to all. Then someone said, "Well, being that we're all here, why don't we say the rosary." Bridget, Hector's wife, led the prayers, and all participated, including Catherine. She started strong with the Creed and the first decade. When they got into the second decade of the beads, Catherine "began to pause now and again as she would lose her place. By the third decade, she was missing a lot." Soon after that, Bridget closed her eyes, a sign to all that Catherine had died. With tears streaming down their faces, the community of Rear Beaver Cove gathered together in the home of John and Maggie Nicholson and finished that rosary "so loud and so clear and so good," because they knew that Catherine MacMullin Nicholson started a rosary with them that night, and by the time it was finished, she was before God.[5]

NICHOLSON. — At the residence of her youngest son, Rear Beaver's Cove, C. B., on the 29th ult., Catherine, relict of the late Alexander Nicholson, at the advanced age of 85 years. Deceased was born at Barra, Scotland, and emigrated to this country 63 years ago. She was beloved and respected by all her acquaintances for her blameless and pious life. Fortified by the last rites of Holy Church, of which she was always a devout member, she peacefully passed away with hope of a glorious resurrection. A large concourse of people followed the remains to their last resting place. She leaves five sons and one daughter to mourn their loss. May her soul rest in peace!

Obituary for Catherine MacMullin Nicholson, The Casket, July 21, 1898. Courtesy of Angus L. MacDonald Library Special Collections, St. F. X. University.

Chapter 10

Hardships

If progress is the life blood of nations it was the death knell of the "Big Glen." Stories of successful men from the neighborhood who were making good away were seeping in. . . . Fame and fortune were beyond the hills and valleys of the "Big Glen." The young became discontented, the old discouraged. By 1910 the "Big Glen" was like the "Deserted Village" of Milton and nature and the forest set in to claim its own.

— P. McE. Nicholson, "The Brothers"

The passing of Big Alex and Catherine Nicholson at the end of the nineteenth century marked a major turning point in Rear Beaver Cove. What was once a vibrant Gaelic community would gradually shed every trace of its simple harmony. As Paddy Nicholson mourned the loss of his beloved grandparents, he recognized that the old ways were on the way out. The farms had nourished them and allowed the children to grow and thrive. The frolics had provided fun and joyful cooperation during some of the more tedious and strenuous tasks. The ceilidhs warmed their hearts on many a blustery winter night. Each resident of this community had put in his full share of labor and love and, in return, received happy and satisfying lives. Land grants were never finalized for many of the pioneers, yet they accomplished the most important goal that had driven them from Barra to Cape Breton in the first place: they answered to no king, no chief, no proprietor or landlord. The work they did was for no one but themselves, on their farm. They worshiped God according to their long-held beliefs in a church that they built together. As idyllic as their lives seemed in 1900, modernity was coming, and it would transform the entire community and the people who lived there.

Modern inventions trickled into the Backlands, making some of the most backbreaking, time-consuming, and monotonous jobs more effortless. "No one unfamiliar with country life can appreciate the extent to which these innovations liberated the farmer and fisherman from drudgery and toil."[1] The loom and the quern became obsolete. Instead, farmers brought their ripened grain to the gristmill and received their flour in a fraction of the time it had once taken. A whole winter's supply could be produced in a day.

Clothing was purchased from Eaton's mail-order catalog. Wearing homespun was looked upon with derision. To take advantage of such time-saving products and services, one needed cash, which was previously unnecessary in a society where everyone produced their food, clothing, and shelter. Yet despite, or perhaps because of, improvements in technology, discontent and discouragement seeped into The Big Glen.

Advertisement in the Halifax Herald, 1904.

First, it was the young men who began to drift away or were sent from the rural farms to urban areas, where they sought employment and sent cash back home to help with the mounting expenses. Even before the turn of the century, as early as the 1870s, a restlessness seemed to infect some of the older boys as they approached manhood. Perhaps they felt a personal responsibility to branch out, earn a living on their own, and provide some extra financial support for their families. My grandfather recognized some of the factors contributing to the exodus from The Big Glen. He said, "The first people, they were satisfied. They brought a generation that helped them have a wonderful country. But that second generation, now and again, one would go and he'd come back well dressed and have a big chain around his vest and jingling in his pocket, and the other young folks that were home, they saw that and they hear the jingling in the pocket and, well, there's a paradise beyond those hills."[2]

Indeed, within the Nicholson family, outmigration began with the second generation. The older sons of Big Alex and Catherine were the first to strike out on their own. In 1871, Old John was a widower living with his parents in Rear Beaver Cove, having lost his first wife and a daughter. Within a few years, he moved to Cape North in Victoria County on the far northeastern shore of Cape Breton. This was a fishing community, and Old John became a foreman at the Challoner fish-processing plant. He married Mary Petrie from Cape North, and they had one son, whom they called Johnny. The young man died in a tragic drowning accident on Aspy Bay at the age of nineteen in 1894. Andrew Dunphy, a neighbor of Old John and Mary, wrote an obituary verse for the grieving parents.[3]

Big John, the second son of Big Alex and Catherine, left the Backlands and moved to Sydney Mines, where he married Lizzie MacDonald in 1879 and became a coal miner. The couple had at least three children. One of them, a daughter named Mary Jessie, married William F. Keefe and raised a family of seven children in the Boston area.

Over the years, as first young men and then young families left Rear Beaver Cove, those who remained bore the burden of growing hardships that weighed down their spirits. Transportation was particularly difficult. Roads were poor, little more than paths or trails through dense forests. Travel between communities was tough; transporting farm products to and from markets in the urban centers was tougher still. The church was six miles away, but getting to Mass on Sundays and Holy Days of Obligation was a high priority. In winter, when the trails were packed down with snow, horse-drawn sleighs glided atop the slick surfaces; at other times, when the rutted trails were sloppy with mud, the trip to church was arduous.

Completion of the intercolonial railroad through Cape Breton in the 1880s was a welcome improvement since it ran along the shoreline of the Bras d'Or Lake from the Canso Straight to Sydney through Beaver Cove and Boisdale. Many of the men living in these Frontland communities got jobs building and working on the railroad. They, in turn, often hired Backland residents to work on their farms at the busiest times. The railroad employees received regular paychecks for their labor; their farm workers from the Backlands were not so fortunate.

Many of the families in the Backlands were large, placing heavy demands on the land to provide sustenance for all. After a long winter during which food stores were depleted, springtime often posed a serious threat of hunger for everyone in Rear Beaver Cove. My grandfather recalled his grandmother telling him how she came to the rescue on one special Tuesday in late February.

Shrove Tuesday came one year and we had no meat. Granny seemed disappointed but equal to the occasion. It was a cold bright day in midwinter with lots of snow on the ground. Father was cutting firewood in the woods, and Alex [Paddy's older brother] was hauling it home. Well, Granny instructed Alex how to set a snare on a well-beaten rabbit path, which he did and baited it well with strands of oat-grain. Coming home with the very next load, a partridge walked ahead of the load for a good many yards and finally ducked off the path right into the snare. That afternoon and in broad daylight, Alex caught a partridge, a spruce-hen, and two rabbits in the one snare. Grandma had her meat and took it for granted the source that supplied it.[4]

* * *

My grandfather entered his teenage years at the turn of the twentieth century, a time of change in the world, his community, his family, and in himself. He was beginning to take note of the forces of nature around him. The little boy was maturing into a man who delighted in the beauty of the natural world and the human spirit. He was acutely aware of the presence of God in the hills and forests, streams, valleys, and lakes of Rear Beaver Cove. Perhaps it was during this coming-of-age time when he first named his surroundings The Big Glen. He must have spent many hours along the shore of his cherished Loon Lake. The stories he wrote often centered around the land of his boyhood, and he described Loon Lake as "*The* Lake, generally understood when people spoke of mysterious happenings, ghosts and fore-runners."[5]

As children approach their teenage years, they often turn to peers for support and friendship. I suspect that it would not have been much different in my grandfather's time. Paddy had close relationships with his older brother, Alex, and particularly his younger brother, Dan. He grew up in close contact with his many cousins, especially the children of his uncles George and Hector. Paddy developed an especially strong admiration and respect for George's son, Patrick J. Nicholson, whose nickname was Pat. Each experienced his changing environment in his own way and followed separate paths into adulthood as a result.

Paddy and Pat Nicholson must have been playmates as kids, wandering the trails of Rear Beaver Cove, hiding behind trees, jumping over brooks, and making their way to the shores of Loon Lake. Maybe they skimmed stones over the surface of the calm lake and watched the reflection of passing clouds on lazy summer afternoons. Although they shared the same first name and were born just two months apart in July and September of 1887, they could not have been more different in their personalities and interests. Paddy loved words, stories, and poetry. He noticed minute details in his natural world. He marveled at the variations in the colors of leaves and grasses as they matured during the year, from the fairest light green of springtime to the splendid deep hues of orange, red, and yellow in the autumn. His cousin Pat was more analytical, mathematical, and scientific in his thinking and in how he looked at the natural world. Yet both Patricks were firmly devoted to God and their shared Catholic faith. They saw the goodness of their heavenly Father everywhere.

They both started school in a single-room schoolhouse. It was there that they began to learn English, how to spell and read, not in their native Gaelic but in the language of the city folk of Cape Breton. They appreciated their Gaelic culture, but they understood that future opportunities might demand a knowledge of English. Still, they spoke Gaelic at home and the cousins conversed with each other in Gaelic as they explored The Big Glen.

A thirst for learning was infused into the collective consciousness of this rural Cape Breton community. Pat Nicholson's mother, Catherine (née Johnston) had been raised in a family that valued education and understood that excellence in learning could not be left to chance. It would require the expenditure of capital. Father A. J. MacMullin, in his magnificent book, *To the Hill of Boisdale*, tells the story of Sarah Shaw, the grandmother of Catherine Johnston Nicholson and great-grand-mother of Pat.[6]

Sarah Shaw was the daughter of a wealthy man, a laird in Scotland, and a Protestant. After becoming a widow at a young age, she married a Catholic man, Roderick Johnston from Barra. Her conversion to Catholicism angered her father, and he disowned her. So Roderick and Sarah Johnston emigrated to Cape Breton with many other Barra inhabitants on the *Harmony* in 1821, and the Johnston family settled in Beaver Cove.

Many years later upon his deathbed, Sarah's father had a change of heart and decided to include his daughter in his inheritance. Much effort was made to locate her, and through inquiries with the government in Sydney, a substantial sum of about five hundred pounds was delivered by boat to the beach at Beaver Cove. Sarah and her family chose to use the fortune to start a school for the children of the community and set in motion a plan to find a suitable teacher. About that time, an English warship arrived in the port of Sydney. One of the passengers was a young aristocratic man, who had been sent by his parents into military service for training in discipline and diligence. Military service was not to his liking, so the young man took the opportunity to jump ship and made his way over-land to Beaver Cove. He was welcomed into the community and recognized as a learned man. They hired him and "fixed up some place for the children to gather and he turned out to be a remarkable teacher. . . . There were many descendants of these people in these schools who went on for education later . . . a whole lot of people who had a respect for education that was created in that community through that teacher, so that the legacy of Sarah Shaw extends all the way down to the present day!"[7]

* * *

As long as enough children were living in the district, each community ensured that they would have a school to attend. These were one-room buildings with a pot-bellied stove in the middle of the classroom. Long desks accommodating three or four pupils on benches were arranged in rows facing the teacher.[8] Girls and boys of all ages learned together in the same classroom, progressing at their own pace. Often, the teacher, whose only qualifications might have been going through a few years of schooling themselves, stayed at the school for only one term. One prospective teacher, when asked why he should be given the job, declared, "Well, I can write the letter, and I can read the letter, and I can send the letter anywhere!"[9] That answer was satisfactory and he was hired on the spot.

The pupils studied mathematics, spelling, and writing, but the high priority was reading. The reading exercises were in English, and for these youngsters, it was their first exposure to the language. They learned Gaelic at their mother's knee, but English would be required for jobs in the cities. They didn't realize it at the time, in 1900, but they would soon seek jobs in Sydney or Boston or Upper Canada. Fluent English was required to get those jobs. The Gaelic had served them well in rural Cape Breton, but the world would demand an English-speaking workforce.

Children did not always have the luxury of attending school regularly, because the demands of subsistence farm life often required everyone, especially strapping young fellows, to work at home. Not every parent shared the same conviction that a child's time is best spent learning to read English or spell R-E-M-A-R-K-A-B-L-E or solve ridiculous arithmetic problems. How many mornings did my grandfather wake up excited about the prospect of another day in the one-roomed school with his teacher, Mike MacIsaac, only to be disappointed because his father had other plans for his time? In his old age, my grandfather reflected on the schooling that he had craved. You could hear the yearning in his voice, and your heart would break for the boy who felt he was "grudged" for even the short amount of time he spent in the simple classroom.[10]

Roddie F. Nicholson, who was three years older than his cousin Paddy, completed nine grades of school in Rear Beaver Cove before Paddy started. One of his teachers even held a bachelor's degree. Roddie passed the provincial exams after he finished his last year. *I thought I was the King of England*, he told his cousins as they reflected on their school days many years later. "You should be in Ottawa, Roddie!" they all remarked.[11]

John D. MacKinnon was a respected schoolmaster in Beaver Cove. He'd made a career teaching children, so he recognized academic and intellectual potential when he saw it. My grandfather's cousin Pat Nicholson came to the attention of Mr. MacKinnon because of his outstanding performance at school in Rear Beaver Cove. The teacher approached Pat's father, George. *Your son is very bright, might I say brilliant. He would benefit from the opportunity to further his education in the city. We cannot provide the lessons here in the rural school that will prepare him for university. He is a serious young fellow and if given the chance, I believe he will make something of himself.*

This conversation did not fall on deaf ears. George may not

have gone to school, but in the 1870s, he learned the carpenter trade as an apprentice in the Boston States. He returned to Rear Beaver Cove to marry and raise a family. As a builder and carpenter, he could earn higher wages working in a city. There, his son Pat could attend grammar and high school. George and his wife Catherine were certainly well aware of their son's scholastic aptitude and they were receptive to the idea that he could distinguish himself if given the opportunity. Did they know at that time, before deciding to leave the Backlands, that there were sponsors who had committed to underwrite the cost of university tuition for Cape Breton boys at St. F. X.? In any case, they decided that Pat must continue his schooling at St. Joseph's school in North Sydney. The census records show that Pat had attended school in the Boisdale district for only two months in 1901. He must have completed that school year in North Sydney, where his father was building a house on Archibald Avenue. By 1902, George, Catherine, and their children moved into that home, and young Pat started on his path to academic excellence.[12]

The one-room school in Rear Beaver Cove was an early casualty of the declining population in the Backlands. As young families left the rural areas around the turn of the century, the small school in Rear Beaver Cove was forced to close its door. The community could not afford a teacher for the few students still living in the district. For my grandfather, who had achieved three grades during the one year he attended school, this was a bitter pill to swallow. Unlike his cousin Roddie, who made nine grades at the little one-room schoolhouse, and Pat, who continued his studies in North Sydney, Paddy Nicholson had no alternative but to drop out after 1901. In one year of formal education, Paddy learned to read and write. That year gave him all the tools he needed to continue his education informally for the remainder of his life.

In 1903, Roddie's father Hector moved his family from Rear Beaver Cove down the hill to Beaver Cove—the Frontland.[13] Hector was suffering from what was then called dyspepsia, a condition that made him too weak to undertake many of the responsibilities of farming. Instead, he kept busy making axe handles and other farm implements. In Beaver Cove, Roddie taught himself the skills necessary to become the district blacksmith, a position vacated upon the death of Alasdair Neill Gobha.[14] He shod horses and forged agricultural tools and implements, common household objects, wagon wheels, and any number of useful items. He was also a good Gaelic singer and an excellent fiddler.

The diaspora from Gaelic communities like Rear Beaver Cove accelerated during the first two decades of the twentieth century. My grandfather's family was not the last to leave, but it took a few years for Paddy's father, Young John, to decide where to settle. He tried working with his brother, Old John, in the fishing industry at Cape North but returned to the Backlands before considering where to go next.[15]

The rapid growth in the population of Cape Breton's industrial cities reflected the expectation that there was money to be made in an economy booming as a result of the worldwide demand for coal. North Sydney had a deep harbor and was growing rapidly as a shipping locus. The collieries of Sydney Mines, Glace Bay, Dominion, and Port Morien attracted miners and ancillary workers. A new steel mill opened in Sydney in 1901. I imagine Paddy and his brothers Alex and Dan peppered their father with questions about their family's future. Considering his options, Young John recognized that farmers are always at the mercy of Mother Nature. One bad year can lead to disaster. *We couldn't leave the farm as long as the old folks were still living with us. But now that they're gone, we can set our sights on finding work in the city. There are plenty of jobs in*

*Glace Bay and Sydney for men willing to work. I guess it will
just be a matter of time.*

That time came in 1907. Young John, his wife Maggie, sons
Paddy and Dan, and their sister Jessie settled down in Glace
Bay, the heart of Cape Breton's coal mining industry. It was the
right place at the right time for a young man like my grandfather, looking for his place in the world.

Paddy's older brother Alex had plans of his own. He and his
cousin, Rory Allan Nicholson, moved to Hamilton, Ontario,
where the two lived within blocks of each other. Rory Allan was
George Nicholson's oldest son, a carpenter and builder like his
father. Perhaps the two young men recognized that their skills
were complementary, and together they could make good
money—carpenter and painter—in a busy city like Hamilton.

Rory Allan married Mary Margaret Martin of Hamilton in
1909, and they raised a family of six children. Alex married a
woman from Cape Breton, Margaret Teresa MacDonnell,
daughter of the Honorable Samuel MacDonnell, a lawyer and
politician from Port Hood. They had two sons and two
daughters.

In 1925, Rory Allan and Alex Nicholson left Canada to
take advantage of a building boom in Miami, Florida. They
entered the United States, leaving wives and children back
home in Ontario. According to the Miami city directory of
1927, the men lived at the same address, and while there, the
city was hit with the worst hurricane in its history on September
17, 1926.

Miami News, Sept. 20, 1926.

The rebuilding of Miami would require the talents of many carpenters and painters, so the cousins found themselves in the right place at the right time. By 1928, however, they returned to their families, Alex to Ontario and Rory Allan to Huntington, New York. Their partnership was over.

I wonder if my grandfather ever saw his older brother after Alex left Cape Breton for Ontario. Would Alex have gotten the news when his parents passed away? Did he return for their funerals? Communication was limited and travel was slow and expensive in the early twentieth century, so there was little if any contact between the brothers. In his recordings, my grandfather spoke with pride about the Nicholson family of Rear Beaver Cove, including family members who had spread all over the country, and all over the world. They had inherited something special from their common ancestors, Big Alex and Catherine from Barra. It would take much more than time and distance to break those bonds.

Chapter 11

A Labor Activist

Nature had been cheated. Her precious gift of fossil fuel intended for the use of all mankind, especially the poor and needy, was now to be exploited to make vast profits for a privileged few.

— John Mellor, "The Company Store"

The origin of the Cape Breton coal mining industry can be traced back 300 million years to a time when the earth was in a prolonged period of global warming. Tropical forests flourished in what is now Cape Breton. Year after year, heavy vegetation growth produced countless layers of decaying organic matter. As the carbon-rich foliage accumulated, underlying layers were compressed into a spongy material called peat, the same substance burned for heat in the hearths of Hebridean blackhouses. Over eons, the weight of these layers compacted the peat beds, fossilizing the carbon-rich material into black, brittle coal—fossil fuel.

In the early stages, the coal lay relatively close to the surface of the earth, but plate tectonics shuffled the continental masses like a deck of playing cards. Massive landforms pushed against each other with unimaginable force. The pressure generated by the collisions buckled the earth's crust, thrusting up great mountain chains along the boundaries. Once-shallow coal deposits were forced down below these mountain chains, further pressurizing them under extreme weight.

Earth's climate and topography are nothing if not evolving, and the tropical earth gradually moderated. By two million years ago, the planet had cooled to the extent that most land masses in the northern hemisphere became snow- and ice-covered and remained so year-round. Glacial rivers captured and stored immense quantities of water, creeping down mountains and across the frozen terrain, scouring everything in their paths. As the Ice Age progressed, heavy accumulations of snow and ice above the coal deposits forced them deeper under the earth's surface, where they lay buried.

Again and over time, the earth's climate gradually warmed, and the Ice Age gave way to increasing temperatures. Glaciers melted and retreated northward, releasing large volumes of water. Sea levels rose and inundated low-lying intercontinental spaces, including the eastern shores of Cape Breton. The climactic shift left a massive reserve of coal extending in long seams under the Atlantic Ocean from the coast of Cape Breton toward the shores of Newfoundland.

The Sydney coalfield is one of the largest of its kind in the world. All that was needed to tap into this energy was the willingness of workers to descend into the mines, cut the coal, and haul it out. It could then work to power coal-burning industries and enrich the mine owners and the government.[1]

* * *

Before 1890, there were just a few small independently-owned coal mining operations along the eastern shores of Cape Breton. The coal extracted from these mines was shipped to the United States and Europe from the ports of Glace Bay and North Sydney. However, during the winter months when these harbors were packed with ice, coal shipments ceased and mining operations ground to a halt. Companies laid off miners and the government lost royalty payments from the sale of coal. The Cape Breton coal industry stagnated without the ability to produce and ship coal year-round.

It was around 1890 that a local Sydney businessman, A.C. Ross, proposed a remedy for this impasse. He approached an American financier, H. W. Whitney, whose manufacturing operations in Boston required an abundant supply of bituminous coal. Together they devised a plan to construct a twenty-mile-long railroad line from the coal fields around Glace Bay to the harbor at Louisburg, which remained ice-free even in winter. From Louisburg, Cape Breton coal could be shipped in any season. In addition, Ross and Whitney proposed amalgamating all of the small mines into one large company, a business with a monopoly on coal mining operations in the Sydney coal fields. The provincial government of Nova Scotia agreed to the scheme, permitting the formation of what became known as the Dominion Coal Company. The company was granted a ninety-nine-year lease beginning in 1894. Glace Bay (from the French *baie de glace*), so named because of the sea ice that formed each winter in its harbor, became home to the company, its miners, and their families.[2]

Among the coal miners were sons of the Scottish settlers who left their land grant farms along the shores of the Bras d'Or Lake. Industrial Cape Breton also attracted waves of immigrants from Scotland and other European countries. These miners needed housing close to the collieries where they worked creating a building boom, attracting even more laborers from rural regions of Cape Breton. Builders and tradesmen likewise needed housing, and so the population of Glace Bay grew rapidly, from about 2500 in 1891 to 16,500 by 1911. Amidst this influx came the family of Young John Nicholson from Rear Beaver Cove in 1907.

Before 1907, Young John spent time searching for the right opportunity for himself and his family outside of Rear Beaver Cove. For a time, he worked in the fishing industry with his brother, Old John, in Cape North. He may have encouraged sons Paddy and Dan to explore their options in the industrial areas around Sydney and Glace Bay whenever they weren't needed on the farm. Many young men living in Cape Breton's rural districts in the early years of the twentieth century traveled by train into the cities to earn some extra cash. Eventually, Young John was hired by the Dominion Coal Company as a carpenter in the machine shop, and his family moved out of the Backlands to Glace Bay.

Whether or not Paddy and Dan had spent any time working in the city before 1907, the move from Rear Beaver Cove to Glace Bay must have been daunting for everyone in the family. The world was changing. They were leaving a life of freedom, self-sufficiency, and neighbor-help-neighbor in search of the prosperity they believed they would find in the urban economy. Yet, Paddy also believed that the values that guided their lives in the Backlands must not be left back on the farm. In Rear Beaver Cove, neighbors could always be trusted to keep their word, lend a hand, and do honest work to support their families and contribute to the community. He may have wondered if those who ran the coal mines in Glace Bay were similarly trustworthy. Did the politicians governing the industrial cities have the best interests of their constituents in mind when making laws that affected the workers and their families? These thoughts began to weigh on Paddy's mind in the weeks and months after he left the Backlands and settled into the new family home on Union Street in Glace Bay.

Paddy's brother Dan was seventeen when the family arrived in the city. He got a job with the S&L Railway working on the trams that provided transportation within and between the industrial cities.

Paddy found a job with an insurance agency, advertising his services in the local newspaper. He distinguished himself by using his mother's maiden name as his middle name. In addition to his work at the agency, P. McE. Nicholson became a reporter for the same newspaper. And there

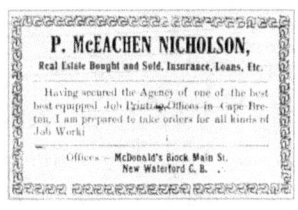

Advertisement in the Glace Bay Standard, May 25, 1911.

was plenty of news to report in the years following the Nicholson family's arrival in town.

Glace Bay was becoming the epicenter of a burgeoning labor movement in Cape Breton. The coal mines were in production all year so miners could count on steady pay. But they could also count on dangerous work conditions and excessively long workdays of twelve hours or more. To help make ends meet, many large families had to send their children, boys as young as nine or ten, to work in the mines.

The Dominion Coal Company created an environment where its miners gradually became completely dependent upon it for survival. They constructed housing for miners and their families around the collieries. Miners rented these small "company houses" from Dominion, and the rent was deducted from their pay. The company also owned and operated a store, stocked with abundant food supplies, household goods, and fine clothing. Families could make purchases at the store on credit, encouraging impulsive and indulgent buying. It was not unusual for a worker to open his pay envelope at the end of a long week to see that every penny of his hard-earned wages had already been spent on the rent and purchases at the company store. Through this vicious cycle, miners fell in over their heads in debt to their employer. Many found it impossible to see their way out of the hole, leading to resentment and despair.

Labor Unions

Before 1908, there was one labor union representing the interests of Cape Breton miners in dealing with their employer, the Dominion Coal Company. The Provincial Workmen's Association or PWA as it was known, had been created in 1879 through a charter of the provincial government to improve "the condition of members morally, mentally and socially."[3] In practice, however, the leadership of this union was tightly linked to the company owners and management as well as the provincial government. The PWA discouraged confrontation between miners and the company. For the most part, this arrangement had been satisfactory in the early years. However, as the Dominion Coal Company strove to remain profitable for its shareholders and to maintain a competitive advantage in the industry, it had to export coal to the United States at prices below market rate. The price of American-produced coal reflected the fact that it was mined by workers organized into strong labor unions like the United Mine Workers of America (UMW), which bargained effectively for higher pay and better work conditions for its miners. In contrast to their American counterparts, Cape Breton miners were subjected to pay cuts and excessively long work days, and the PWA was unwilling and unable to negotiate any sort of satisfactory relief.

So pressure began to mount among the miners for a stronger union, one that would more forcefully represent the miners' interests. Perhaps Cape Breton miners could organize under a charter of the UMW. A sizable contingent of the workforce was anxious to accept them. When a representative from the UMW headquarters in Indianapolis came to speak in Cape Breton, his message resonated with many of the miners. The Dominion Coal Company, however, was dead set against it, believing that the UMW would jeopardize its advantageous position in the American coal market. So the company fought against the UMW in Cape Breton. Nevertheless, by the spring of 1909, the PWA split into two factions, and about half of the miners joined the UMW. The fissure led to "bitter acrimony and distrust," experienced not only in the mines but also within the homes of miners where father and son, or brothers, were often members of competing unions.[4]

Articles, letters, and editorials in local newspapers sought to influence public attitudes toward labor unions. The *Glace Bay Standard* was sympathetic to labor, supporting miners who agitated for higher wages and better work conditions. The *Sydney Post,* in contrast, warned that a strike by the miners against the coal company would bring devastating consequences to the whole community.

The office of the *Glace Bay Standard* was on Union Street, near the home of P. McE. Nicholson and his family. As a reporter for the *Standard,* he wrote about the negotiations between labor leaders and Dominion Coal Company representatives. He had been present for confrontations that developed when miners walked out and set up picket lines. He interviewed miners and their union leaders. He witnessed the growing despair of the workers through the spring and early summer of 1909, with no improvements in pay or work conditions. When negotiations inevitably broke down between the coal company and UMW, their only recourse was to strike. By early July, it was clear that whatever the consequences, UMW members would stand together. The strike date was set for July 6.

Only UMW miners walked out of the mine that day; PWA union members remained on the job, crossing the UMW picket lines. The division between UMW and PWA in the mines was reflected in the homes, where members of the same family could be affiliated with different unions. Paddy later recalled, "Conditions were terrible. . . . Father and son would oppose one another, two brothers opposing one another, and labor was divided. There was a very bad feeling among the miners."[5]

The No. 2 mine in New Aberdeen was the largest in the area. It had miners in both the UMW and the PWA. If the strike by UMW miners was going to be successful in stopping the operations of Dominion Coal, then New Aberdeen would be the bellwether. Located about a mile from Paddy Nicholson's home, it was a short walk to the pit head for the young reporter that eventful morning of July 6. He would have heard the commotion coming from the agitated miners pacing and chanting around the entrance to the New Aberdeen mine. The prediction of a picket force of about 700 miners was shattered by the actual turnout.

Major Canadian and American newspapers picked up the story and described the scene on the morning of July 6. Under the headlines, "Violence is Coming," the Montreal Gazette reported,

> Dominion No. 2, the recognized stronghold of the U.M.W. proved as predicted, to be the storm center of the strike.
>
> From early morning hundreds of men began gathering about the fence that surrounds this mine, and by evening upwards of 3,000 miners had congregated here. . . . From 3 to

6 o'clock they kept lined up at the main entrance of the colliery, and the workmen as they left the plant were compelled to pass through a long lane of strike sympathizers, three and four deep, who launched taunting cries of 'scab, scab' at the outcoming men.[6]

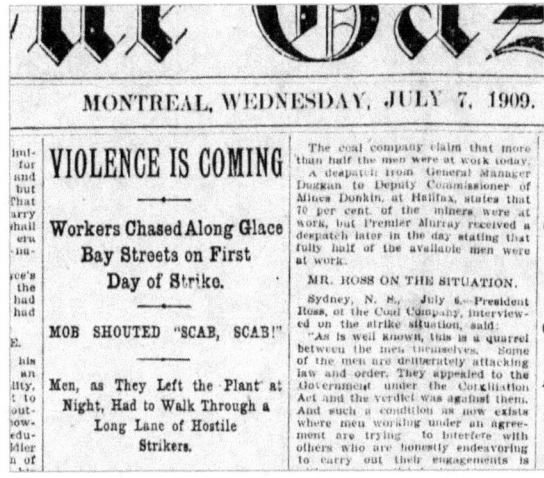

MONTREAL, WEDNESDAY, JULY 7, 1909.

VIOLENCE IS COMING

Workers Chased Along Glace Bay Streets on First Day of Strike.

MOB SHOUTED "SCAB, SCAB!"

Men, as They Left the Plant at Night, Had to Walk Through a Long Lane of Hostile Strikers.

The coal company claim that more than half the men were at work today. A despatch from General Manager Duggan to Deputy Commissioner of Mines Donkin, at Halifax, states that 70 per cent. of the miners were at work, but Premier Murray received a despatch later in the day stating that fully half of the available men were at work.

MR. ROSS ON THE SITUATION.

Sydney, N. S., July 6.—President Ross, of the Coal Company, interviewed on the strike situation, said: "As is well known, this is a quarrel between the men themselves. Some of the men are deliberately attacking law and order. They appealed to the Government under the Conciliation Act and the verdict was against them. And such a condition as now exists where men working under an agreement are trying to interfere with others who are honestly endeavoring to carry out their engagements is

The Montreal Gazette, July 7, 1909, page 1.

Paddy knew that the company had warned the UMW that miners who failed to show up for work would be evicted immediately from their company homes. The union arranged to have canvas tents delivered to the area to provide shelter for those evicted families. But those temporary dwellings would prove inadequate if the strike continued into the cruel winter months. And continue it did.

Eviction. The horror of it struck home for Paddy. It was at the heart of the exile endured by his grandparents. It was the reason for their emigration from Barra. He knew well of the cruelty they suffered at the hands of greedy landlords, forcefully evicting the Gaels from their homes. Now Paddy could see for himself the inhumanity of greedy mine owners as they threw their employees out on the street. Coming home, night after night for months, he watched helplessly as company police entered homes and took out all the families' possessions—their furniture, their clothes, and all their food. They just dumped it all into the gutter. Then they locked them out of their homes. The poor souls had nowhere to go.

I can imagine the conversation around the supper table as Paddy told his family what he had seen in New Aberdeen that day. *Father Fraser was going along the street offering each of these poor, destitute miners' families a chance to move into the church, the school, or the rectory.*[7]

Maggie Nicholson would have understood how these events troubled her son. *Paddy, Father Fraser is a holy and humble man. His parishioners love him for his compassion and kindness. Do you wonder how long he will be able to support the striking miners and their families by giving them shelter in the parish buildings?*

That is the problem, Mumma, Paddy said. *Alec MacNeil, the Grand Marshal of the Knights of Columbus in the parish, watched what was going on. He didn't approve, so he traveled to Antigonish to report to Bishop Cameron on what Father Fraser was doing.*

"He told Bishop Cameron that the coal company was not only fighting the PWA and the United Mine Workers, but also the Catholic Church and he lay before him how Father Fraser was bringing in those that they were evicting. Father Fraser that same evening, that same day, got a telegram from Bishop Cameron to go up, that he wanted to see him, and without going back to New Aberdeen, was put in a parish up in Antigonish county. [The striking] men immediately were told to leave the property of the parish of New Aberdeen."[8]

Paddy knew that with the departure of Father Fraser, the

miners and their families would again be out on the street. He wondered how the Bishop could, in good conscience, take the side of the Dominion Coal Company. Maggie may have expected this incident to embitter her son to the Church, yet she would come to understand that such experiences only strengthened his commitment to his faith.

As the strike continued through the summer of 1909 and well into fall and winter, The *Glace Bay Standard* covered the story and stressed the viewpoints of striking miners. Articles explaining how and why the strike began, directed at the company executives, fell on deaf ears. At the same time, conditions in the tent city around the collieries deteriorated along with the changing weather. Sanitation was non-existent, so diseases, including cholera, typhoid, scarlet fever, diphtheria, tuberculosis, influenza, and pneumonia, began to spread. Paddy remembered that "Conditions were so bad that one shank of beef with this big bone in it went from house to house for about twenty-one days, each one boiling it for soup but nobody ever put a knife on a bit of the meat that was on that shank, that's how conditions were."[9] Babies and children bore the brunt of these highly contagious illnesses, and most of the evicted families were impacted.

The coal company continued to fend off efforts by strike leaders to obtain official recognition from the UMW. By April 1910, the local chapter was forced to admit defeat and end the strike that had caused so much pain and suffering in the community of Glace Bay. However, P. McE. Nicholson's work at The *Glace Bay Standard* during the strike established his reputation as a labor sympathizer, one who divulged the worker's plight to the general public through the power of the press.

Lily

Lily, this is my Mumma. You can call her Mumma, too. Paddy bent over and gently led the toddler into the kitchen. The child must have been no more than three, and the tears that streaked down her dirty face betrayed her fear and insecurity.

Maggie Nicholson glanced with disbelief from her son to little Lily Smith. She bent over until she was face to face with the child, and quietly asked, *Lily, have you had anything to eat today?* It was already late afternoon, but the child just looked down at her bare feet and shook her head slowly. Maggie lifted her onto a chair at the kitchen table, opened the small cupboard in the corner of the room, and took out a pan of bannock. Pulling a large piece off the end of the loaf, she tore it in half and spread each side with a generous slab of soft butter. Then she looked up at Paddy, and, choosing her words carefully, inquired, *Have you seen Mrs. Smith today?* He motioned for his mother to follow him out the back door, where they spoke in hushed tones.

Paddy told his mother the terrible news that Lily's mother died yesterday. She was a young woman, married to Edmund Smith who served in the armed forces. *Her father is not going to be able to take care of her. You know he'll have to be away most of the time. Her sister, Winnie, is going off to live with her grandmother in England. The two little ones will have to go into the orphanage, but I'd hate to see them put Lily in there, too, Mumma. She needs a good home. Can we not take her in?*

Maggie agreed. Lilian J. Smith, though never officially

adopted by Maggie and Young John Nicholson, was raised in their household and treated as a full member of the family.

* * *

On August 4, 1914, England declared war on Germany. As a self-governing dominion of the British Commonwealth, Canada was instantly thrust into the conflict and the country pulled together to support the war effort. Large numbers of young men from Cape Breton, like their counterparts in the rest of the nation, joined the Canadian Expeditionary Force and shipped off to the front in Europe. The strategic value of coal and steel in wartime manufacturing kept the coal mines and steel plant operating at full capacity. Labor unions discovered unprecedented leverage at the bargaining table between 1914 and 1918, the years spanning the First World War. My grandfather recalled, "Labor had to get something. And God knows they needed it."[10]

It was around this time that Young John and Maggie Nicholson pulled up stakes and relocated the family again, moving about twelve miles from Glace Bay to Sydney. Paddy established himself in the business of painting and wallpapering while his commitment to the labor movement in Sydney only deepened. He wrote newspaper columns in support of the workers of Cape Breton, reporting for the *Sydney Record* and the *Canadian Labor Leader*. In 1916, he published a regular weekly newspaper column under the pen name, "A Man in Overalls." In his articles, he argued for the rights of labor, solidifying his reputation as a labor activist in Cape Breton.

Paddy was an active member of the Brotherhood of Painters and Decorators, Local 26, in Sydney. This and other trade unions, such as the Carpenters' and the Postal Workers' unions, together formed the Sydney Trades and Labor Council, a local chapter of the Trades and Labor Congress of Canada (TLC). Every year, the TLC of Canada held a national meeting, with delegates attending from every province. The thirty-third annual convention of the TLC convened in Ottawa, Ontario, the capital of Canada, during the third week of September 1917. Paddy attended as the delegate from Sydney and a member of the convention's Executive Committee. Arriving in Ottawa, my grandfather and the other labor delegates found themselves at the center of a city embroiled in controversy.

The war in Europe raged on into its fourth year. Canadian troop losses were high: 25,000 men before 1917 and another 10,000 that year. Enlistments were not keeping up with losses, and by the end of August, it was becoming painfully clear that stronger measures would be necessary to win the war. Under the leadership of Prime Minister Sir Robert Borden, Parliament passed the *Military Service Bill*, authorizing compulsory military service.

As head of the Conservative party, Sir Robert had been elected Prime Minister in 1911. By 1917, the economy was in terrible shape and Borden's government was unpopular. An election was overdue, but a wartime election was considered unnecessarily divisive when it was important to promote unity throughout the country. So the Prime Minister approached the Liberal opposition leader, Sir Wilfred Laurier, with an offer to form a coalition government. If Laurier agreed, there would be no need for a wartime election. However, Laurier refused; his Liberals were divided over conscription, and he believed that the people should decide the matter at the polls. The election of 1917 would essentially be a referendum on conscription.

Conscription was unpopular, but English-speaking Canadians of both parties were generally supportive of the war effort; French-speaking members of the Liberal party in Quebec were not. Borden sought to take advantage of the division within the

Liberal Party by going straight to members at the Provincial level, inviting them to join a new party, called the Unionist Party, something that had never been done before. As the country prepared for the fall election, candidates would be nominated as either Unionists—a combination of Borden Conservatives and Liberals who supported conscription—or anti-conscription Laurier Liberals. Unionists from the Conservative Party and the Liberal crossovers were promised cabinet positions in the Union government.

Sir Borden found another way to stack the cards in favor of his Unionist party before the election by introducing the *Wartime Elections Act of 1917*. The bill would alter the franchise for certain classes of Canadians, bestowing voting rights on those who favored conscription and denying them to those opposed. At that time, women were generally forbidden to vote in Canada, but the *Wartime Elections Act of 1917* opened the franchise to those women with family members involved in overseas combat. Their ballot would essentially substitute for that of a husband or son while they were out of the country. As these women were likely to be in favor of conscription, their votes would support Unionist candidates. On the other hand, immigrants from hostile countries who were considered to be against conscription were disenfranchised by the Wartime Elections Act.

Finally, the Act would alter several routine election procedures. Nominations, usually occurring a week before the election, were due one month before election day. Additionally, enumerators appointed by members of the Conservative federal government prepared the voter lists.[11] On Thursday, September 20, 1917, Parliament passed the *Wartime Elections Act*.

Meanwhile, across the capital city of Ottawa, the Canadian Trades and Labor Congress convened on Monday, September 17. In attendance was my grandfather representing the Sydney

TLC and a member of the Executive Committee, tasked with bringing to the floor "the most important of the sixty-five resolutions now before the convention."[12] One of the most contentious resolutions stated the position of organized labor concerning the question of conscription. Debate on the resolution began Wednesday, and when the President of the Congress, James C. Watters, asked those opposed to conscription to rise to their feet, only about a half dozen remained seated.

In the final hours of the TLC convention, the delegates nominated officers to serve at the thirty-fourth session in 1918. Then, the convention took up the question of political representation for labor in the upcoming national election. Without a party of its own, Liberal and Unionist candidates would split the labor vote. Labor needed a party that could propose legislation specifically in *its* best interest. The delegates approved a resolution stating, "We therefore strongly recommend the formation of an independent labor party for Canada."[13] It was a recommendation that Paddy Nicholson took very seriously.

Miserable Politics

While attending the TLC, my grandfather met George Kyte, the Liberal M.P. from Richmond County in Cape Breton. Kyte had not joined the Unionist ranks of Sir Robert Borden, instead following the anti-conscription platform of the Laurier Liberals. Paddy later recalled that "He [Kyte] took me into Sir Wilfred Laurier's office and they started telling me about the Wartime Election Act" that was going through Parliament. They explained that, because of the Act, it was almost a sure thing that the Prime Minister, Sir Robert Borden, would be reelected; he had gerrymandered the electorate in favor of his Unionist party. "And besides everything else miserable that was attached to it was the fact that nominations would be held a month ahead of the election, which has never taken place in Canada before or after," Paddy remembered. Unfortunately, there was little labor could do about that.[14]

After returning home from Ottawa, Paddy received a message that George Kyte wished to meet him at the Sydney Hotel. Kyte knew of Paddy's reporting in the labor newspapers and that he attracted a wide readership of voters, particularly anti-conscription labor voters. Kyte began by stating that nominations for the upcoming election would be held next Tuesday, but he was going to be the Liberal candidate from Richmond County. John C. Douglas would be the Unionist candidate.

"Why weren't the people consulted about this?" Paddy asked.

"Oh, the people don't understand," Kyte replied, "and, anyhow, it's better this way."

Stunned by his display of arrogance, Paddy said, "You'll never become a member without the consent of the people of Cape Breton and Richmond."

"Why not?" asked Kyte.

"Because I, for one, will oppose you."

"Well, now, stop. Just wait a minute. I have a job in mind, it pays $150 a week. You can walk right into it by just staying quiet."

If he hadn't realized this before that moment, Paddy understood now very clearly the power of the press. His columns were widely read, and Kyte knew that this young reporter and labor activist had the attention of the workers of Cape Breton through his articles in labor newspapers.

Perhaps Kyte believed that his offer would be irresistible for a man who made little money as a painter and even less as a reporter and union organizer. Without hesitation, Paddy told Kyte, "No, nothing doing." He gathered up his overcoat and turned to leave the room, knowing that he would probably never meet George Kyte again. As disillusioned as he must have been after that meeting, Paddy realized that labor would have to enter the arena of "miserable politics" to achieve its most noble goals. And he knew exactly where to go to enter that arena. He would pay a visit to Dick Harris.

Harris published the *Canadian Labor Leader*, one of the Sydney papers that Paddy edited and contributed to under his pen name, A Man in Overalls. Closing the door to Harris's office, he respectfully asked for a full-page ad in Saturday's issue. Paddy explained that he planned to "write a proclamation calling for a meeting of the labor leaders of Cape Breton County with the object in mind of establishing a Labor Party." True to his word, Harris published the notice in the paper that Saturday.

My grandfather must have been gratified by the response to his advertisement because, on Tuesday, cars arrived at Greenville Hall from as far away as Louisburg in the East and Bras d'Or in the North. As editor of the *Canadian Labor Leader*, P. McE. Nicholson presided over the meeting and made a case for an Independent Labor Party. The two-party system only served to divide labor. "The only time that Labor can come together and at the same time get concessions for itself and for its workers will be when they have a party of their own, and then they will get away from both parties," Nicholson implored those in attendance at that meeting. "This is our one chance to have our own Labor party candidates in the coming election." His impassioned speech convinced those who came from near and far that a Labor Party would be the best way to serve themselves and their families. Time was of the essence, and the attendees moved immediately to form the Independent Labor Party of Cape Breton. They elected John C. MacNeil, from the carpenter's union in Sydney, as Chairman of the party and Jim McLaughlin of Glace Bay as Secretary-Treasurer.[15]

Next, the members turned to the nomination process to select candidates to run in the upcoming election: Robert Baxter from Glace Bay and John Gillis from Sydney. They all knew that the task ahead was colossal, but if they could just convince enough voters to support the Labor candidates, the result could be revolutionary.

The majority of the population of Cape Breton lived outside the industrial areas on farms and in fishing villages. It would take more time than they had to demonstrate the worthiness of the Labor candidates to those voters who may not have any understanding of the Labor Party's platform.

Unfortunately, the first election in which the Independent Labor Party ran candidates in Cape Breton South and Richmond counties was too little too late. "We lost, we lost our deposit of $200 each, we were a little in debt, but we could write it off. Well, the year afterward we elected four labor men to the Province of Nova Scotia and beat some of the strongest Liberals and strongest Conservatives in the country," Paddy boasted years later.[16] God knows the struggle had been well worth it.

* * *

The Sydney steel plant opened in 1901, producing railroad rails and employing hundreds of steelworkers, whose early attempts to organize fell flat when the company refused to recognize the union. Even when members of the PWA invited steel workers to join their union in 1904, the arrangement failed and it took another thirteen years before steel workers attempted to unionize on their own. Emboldened by the success of the UMW on behalf of Glace Bay miners, Sydney steel workers found their voices and organized in 1917. My grandfather played a role in the successful endeavor.

The United Mine Workers put an ad in the Sydney papers that they were coming in here . . . a certain night with the object of organizing the steel workers, and that they would stand behind them at the piers and in the mines if they would [organize], so they advertised . . . to hold a meeting. They came in, I was there, but instead of having a few, the school field down here, it was full of people. They were anxious, they were thirsty to join, and Alexander Hall wouldn't hold a quarter of them. So we started looking for a hall, we wanted to rent the Lyceum, and I [went] looking for Hugh MacAdam [who leased out] the Lyceum. I couldn't find him, so we went down to the Lyceum and I broke a dollar and a quarter lock that was on the door, and let in the men, and they organized that night. [They organized] as steelworkers and made application for a charter.[17]

That would be the end of Paddy's involvement with the steelworkers union, at least for a while.

* * *

The First World War came to an end with the armistice on November 11, 1918. Canada had paid a heavy toll, mourning the deaths of 66,000 men and over 120,000 wounded. Overall, more than nine million soldiers died and more than twenty-one million more were wounded. Known at the time as The Great War because of the scale and scope of the devastation, it was called "the war to end all wars." Sadly, this designation proved to be short-lived.

My grandfather continued working as a painter and a labor activist throughout 1918. He continued editing and writing columns for the *Canadian Labor Leader*. He was instrumental in organizing unions in and around Sydney for various labor groups, including steam fitters, coal haulers, and clerks. With each new union that he formed, he was paid about $20. It wasn't much but every little bit helped, as the economy plunged into a recession after the war ended in November 1918.

P. McE. Nicholson's involvement in the Cape Breton labor movement would soon be interrupted by new developments within his family. However, his heart remained firmly committed to the cause. Although he was officially out of the labor movement by 1920, his reputation was known in the area, and sometimes he was able to take advantage of that notoriety on behalf of union members who needed help. One day in 1923, after the settlement of a strike that shut down coal and steel works in Sydney, he ran into a neighbor who had been blacklisted from his job at the steel plant.[18]

"Why aren't you working?" Paddy asked his friend.

"I can't. There's so many of us blacklisted that we will never get work at the plant," he replied in despair.

"Where's the union? What is the union doing for you?" Paddy asked.

"They said they cannot do a thing. We lost, and there's nothing we can do," the man stated.

Well, Paddy got interested in this situation and he hunted down the secretary-treasurer of the Steelworker's Union, a man by the name of Campbell.

"What are you doing for those men that were blacklisted and can't get back to work?"

Campbell shook his head. "I'm sorry that those men have been let go. But we're lucky that so many of us *are* working."

"Well, that's not going to feed the children of the people that are out. Can't you do something?" Paddy asked.

"No, we cannot do a thing," said Campbell.

"Alright, then, I'm going to try," said Paddy, never one to take "No" for an answer. He sent a telegram to Dan Cameron, the provincial secretary in Halifax, asking for an appointment. After receiving word that Cameron would meet him at nine o'clock the next morning and using his own money, he went to Halifax, traveling by train that night and arriving early the next morning. He walked around the streets until the appointed time and entered the secretary's office.

"So what brings you here this morning, Mr. Nicholson?" asked Cameron.

Paddy began by explaining that 129 steelworkers had been blacklisted by the company in Sydney because they had taken part in the strike. They would never be allowed back into their former plant; now they were going to have to leave Nova Scotia to find work.

"Your father was a Presbyterian and came from Scotland. My grandfather was a Catholic and he also came from Scotland. They came from Scotland not because they wanted to leave but because they had to. They were driven away," Paddy said. "The same situation is taking place in Cape Breton this very minute. There are people in Cape Breton, Scotch Catholic and Scotch Protestants, that's gotta leave their homes, same as our forefathers did, because they are driven away," he said. "I came up to see you because the Dominion Steel Company's workers are working under a charter of the provincial government. You're the provincial secretary. I want to know what you're going to do about it?"

"Alright," Cameron said, reaching for the telephone on his desk. He dialed the number for D. H. MacDougall in New Glasgow. "I am Dan Cameron, the provincial secretary. Well, there's a number of men, 129 to be exact, who have been blacklisted in Sydney by your company. I want those people back tomorrow morning." After Cameron hung up the phone, he turned to the man waiting in his office. "You're all right, Pat. You can go right home. They will be working tomorrow."

And by the time Paddy returned to Sydney on the train, the blacklisted men had been called back to work. After all the years, all the ups and downs, failures and successes large and small, there could be little doubt in Paddy's mind that it had all been more than worthwhile, not only for himself but for the many miners, steel workers, tradesmen and their families whose quality of life improved as a result of the efforts of a Man in Overalls.

* * *

During the time that my grandfather was devoting himself to the Cape Breton labor movement, between 1907 and 1920, his cousin Patrick J. Nicholson devoted himself to his studies. His parents, George and Catherine, had left Rear Beaver Cove in 1902, moving their family to North Sydney. Young Pat completed his secondary education at St. Joseph's High School in North Sydney by 1905. He turned eighteen years old that September and would have been looking toward the future to study at university, perhaps beyond.

St. Francis Xavier University in Antigonish celebrated its fiftieth anniversary in 1905. Such milestones are opportunities for institutions to reflect upon past accomplishments and establish goals for the future. Such was the case for St. F. X.'s leadership that year. The administration knew that progress had been made at the school during the first half-century, and they believed that St. F. X. could soon be recognized as *the premier* Catholic university in Canada. However, it would be necessary to build upon the strength of their faculty and to produce educated professors, not only in the classics and humanities but just as importantly in the sciences.[19]

Perhaps, in part, it was a matter of being in the right place at the right time for Patrick J. Nicholson, as he prepared to begin university in 1905. While tuition and fees at St. F. X. were modest by many standards, the university had identified sponsors who wished to finance the educational expenses for promising young men. At the time, few students were interested in pursuing a career in science, but Pat, as he was called, distinguished himself by his intention to study physics. At university, he worked hard and demonstrated his ability as a serious and brilliant student. In 1909, the year that my grandfather reported on the coal miner's strike in Glace Bay, his cousin graduated from St. F. X. with a bachelor's degree in Physics.

Pat Nicholson was among a select group of graduates that year sent to renowned institutions around the world to further their studies. Pat went to Johns Hopkins University in Baltimore, Maryland, where he earned his Masters and Ph.D. degrees in physics in 1912. Upon returning to Antigonish, Doc Pat began teaching in the physics department at St. F. X.

By the next academic year, he had discerned a calling to the priesthood. In 1913, he entered the Grand Seminary in Montreal for one year before transferring to St. Augustine's Seminary in Toronto. He was ordained at St. Basil's Cathedral in Toronto on June 29, 1916.[20] He returned to St. F. X. as Father Patrick J. Nicholson. By 1920, as his cousin Paddy Nicholson was withdrawing from the labor movement in Sydney, Father Pat was building his reputation as a professor and scientist in Antigonish. His contributions to the success of St. F. X. would soon be recognized by many in Nova Scotia and beyond.

Chapter 12

Sydney

There is something magnificent about a man in overalls ... He is the incarnation of the social revolution — a mighty disturber of the peace.

— Eugene V. Debs, 1912

My grandfather turned thirty in July 1917. He had matured into a very different person than the wide-eyed young man who'd arrived in Glace Bay ten years earlier. Although life in Rear Beaver Cove had its hardships and challenges, Paddy found Glace Bay an altogether different world. He had witnessed the earliest days of the Cape Breton labor movement, as workers discovered that their voices were amplified by banding together for a common cause. When strikes became necessary, workers endured other indignities. Many were evicted from their company homes or were black-listed from ever working again in their community. In his work as an activist and a reporter, P. McE. Nicholson—A Man in Overalls—had left his mark on the Cape Breton labor move-ment. In return, the labor movement had left a mark on him. He became a champion of the underdog. He empathized with people who were down on their luck and he suffered with those who were treated unfairly. He didn't hesitate to intervene on their behalf whenever he was able. For Paddy, it was simply a matter of Christian charity.

One evening, around 1918, my grandfather's life was about to change. I reckon it had something to do with his inclination to seek out individuals who were suffering in silence. Years later, his children remembered the story of how he met their mother at a dance in Sydney. It might have been a church dance, held in the Lyceum, or a benefit dance for the Scottish Gaelic Society or the League of the Cross. In any case, Paddy Nicholson noticed a girl sitting alone in a room full of happy young people. While everyone chatted and laughed waiting for the fiddlers to start playing happy jigs and reels, this young lady was alone and appeared to be crying. No one else paid any attention to her. Of course, Paddy would have been drawn to her, seeing her sadness. Who was this girl, and what could have brought her out to a dance with such a heavy heart? He was going to find out. He couldn't help himself.

Paddy walked nonchalantly over to where she was sitting. She hadn't noticed his approach because her gaze was locked on the floor. She was young, perhaps eighteen or nineteen, much younger than himself. Until now, he hadn't met anyone who interested him. He was preoccupied with his work as a painter and decorator, editor for the *Canadian Labor Leader*, and union organizer. None of these jobs paid enough to support a family, especially at a time when the cost of every necessity of life was rising at a staggering rate. Indeed, he was barely making enough income to do his share in helping his parents maintain their family home.

As he approached, the young lady sensed his presence in front of her. Was it possible that this man had come over to ask her to dance? Couldn't he tell that she was not in a dancing mood? She wished she could just crawl under her seat and become invisible to everyone in the room, including this fellow, but it seemed that it was too late for her to escape his notice.

Before saying anything to her, Paddy began to dance a little jig right in front of her seat in the corner of the room. Dancing had always lightened the mood back in the little Nicholson cabin in Rear Beaver Cove or anywhere else, he found. So he used a silly face and happy feet to try and break the ice with the girl. His strategy was working; as hard as she tried to avoid his attention, she couldn't help but smile at this gangly fellow who must have singled her out in this hall full of happy folks.

And what's your name, then? Paddy asked as he reached down to take her hand and lead her out onto the dance floor. *I'm Paddy Nicholson. My family moved to Sydney about a year ago from Glace Bay. I haven't seen you here at the dances before.*

Hello, Paddy. My name is Annie, Annie MacPherson, she whispered. He had to lean in to hear her soft voice.

Do you live nearby? Are you in Sacred Heart parish? he asked.

I live on Johnston Street with my parents, my sisters, and my brothers. But I'm leaving home. I told them I wouldn't be back. I've had an argument with my father and he's angry with me for leaving. Now I'm not sure where I'm to go after the dance, she explained. Paddy had such a kind look on his face. He seemed to understand exactly what she was feeling, and it was easy to talk to him. God knows she needed someone to listen to her tonight.

Is your father Joseph? Paddy asked. *My brother Dan works on the electric trams with a Joseph MacPherson.* Paddy had never met the man but knew of him through the Trades and Labor Council. Joseph MacPherson was the treasurer of the Street and Electric Employee union while Dan Nicholson served as Secretary. *I suppose Joseph MacPherson knows who I am*, Paddy thought.

Annie nodded, and just then the music started up. They danced together for the rest of the set, and when the band took a break, Paddy returned to the corner with Annie. As they sat down to rest, he wondered if there was some way he could help her.

I'm worried about you leaving home, Annie. It's not safe and you need a place to stay, said Paddy. *Why don't you come home with me? I live with my parents on Douglas Street, not far from here. My sister, Jessie, got married and lives in Glace Bay now, so you can stay in her room tonight. My mother can see that you are comfortable, and we'll talk about your going home tomorrow morning.*

With that, she reluctantly agreed to go home with her new friend. Could either of them have predicted that their meeting at a dance that evening was the start of a relationship that lasted more than fifty years?

* * *

The next morning, when Paddy walked Annie to her home a few blocks away from his own, he was met with the angry words of a protective father.

I want you to stay away from my daughter! Joseph MacPherson bellowed.

Paddy was neither surprised nor offended to hear Mr. MacPherson speak to him in that tone of voice. What caring father would not have? How could Annie's father have known that Paddy was not the sort of person who would take advantage of a young lady under these conditions? Paddy could see that it was going to take time to show Joseph MacPherson and his wife, Sarah, that he only wanted what was best for Annie.

Perhaps Joseph MacPherson had already formed an opinion about Paddy Nicholson based on his activities in the Cape Breton labor movement. Although Paddy wrote his newspaper articles under his pen name, A Man in Overalls, many locals knew that he was a labor activist. Some people believed that all union activists were socialists, with the stigma that such a designation carried. Oftentimes, Paddy felt disapproval, even disdain, from acquaintances and even some family members because of his ideas and writings. If Joseph MacPherson considered Paddy to be a labor agitator, he might look upon him as if he had cloven hooves—the devil himself! Paddy couldn't presume that Annie's father would understand his political ideology, but he could try to earn his approval, someday.

It wouldn't take long until Paddy recognized what a very special young lady he had met at the dance that Saturday night. He would soon appreciate Annie's kindness and her willingness to work tirelessly for the good of her family. Like himself, Annie was devout in her Catholic faith and she shared his beliefs and values. Her ancestors had come to Cape Breton from the tiny Isle of Barra, just like the Nicholson and MacMullin families of Rear Beaver Cove. She grew up in a Gaelic-speaking home and treasured the music, traditions, and hospitality so characteristic of the Gaels of Cape Breton. Indeed, Paddy Nicholson and Annie MacPherson had much in common.

However, in some respects, Paddy and Annie could not have been more different. Perhaps it was their distinct personalities: he, outgoing; she, reserved. Or maybe their earliest childhood experiences set them on paths that would account for their attraction as polar opposites at that dance in Sydney.[1]

* * *

J oseph MacPherson was born around 1860 in Middle Cape near Big Pond, Cape Breton on the 184-acre farm that had been granted to his grandfather Roderick MacPherson in 1836. The land remains in the MacPherson family to this day. Joseph's father Neil R., a farmer and merchant who ran a general store on the road between St. Peter's and Sydney, was well-known and well-liked by his neighbors and many customers.[2]

From an early age, Joseph was expected to take responsibility for his actions. One day, when working with a neighbor to "snake logs from the woods" along a narrow path, a log got hung up, causing the swingletree to break in two. Joseph explained to his father that the horse broke the swingletree, but Neil R. corrected his son's version of events. "Don't blame the horse. . . . You broke the swingletree. Take another one, and this time be careful. You know how you broke the last one, so don't break another one."[3]

Joseph moved to Windham County, Connecticut in 1888. There were good jobs in the granite quarries around Sterling town, attracting immigrants from Cape Breton and other French and English parts of Canada, Poland, Italy, and Scotland. Three MacNeil brothers from Red Islands, a village not far from Middle Cape along the Bras d'Or Lake, worked in the quarries with Joseph. Their sister, Sarah MacNeil, also lived in Sterling with her husband, Michael MacNeil. When Michael died, Sarah was left a widow and the single mother of their infant son. It must have been a relief to Sarah when Joseph MacPherson asked for her hand in marriage. Their wedding took place at All Hallows Church in Moosup, Connecticut on May 11, 1897. Although Sarah's son Michael retained his MacNeil surname, he was adopted by Joseph MacPherson, who raised him as his own.

A daughter was born to Joseph and Sarah on February 17, 1898. They named her Anne after both her maternal (Anne Kennedy) and paternal (Anne Matheson) grandmothers. A second daughter, born in 1901, was named Mary Catherine but my grandmother called her sister Catherine throughout their lives. Annie and Catherine could have been mistaken for twins, alike in disposition and appearance.

It appears that Joseph MacPherson had no intention of staying in the U. S. and becoming an American citizen, for he maintained his alien status throughout the fourteen years that he lived in Connecticut. Shortly after Catherine's birth, Joseph and Sarah moved back to Cape Breton, but not to his ancestral land at Middle Cape. They landed in the growing industrial center of Whitney Pier, the site of the new Sydney steel plant. Between 1890 and 1905 its population grew tenfold. Joseph became a trackman, working on the electric trams for the power company. In October 1903, a son, Neil, was born and another daughter, Mary Anne, arrived in 1908, when Sarah and Joseph were in their mid-forties.

Years later, Joseph was hired by the post office as a mail carrier, taking incoming mail from the train station to the local post office and outgoing mail back to the train depot. In this capacity, Joseph was one of the first in town to drive a motor vehicle.[4] He bought an eight-room home on Johnston Street in Sydney. He had achieved considerable financial success, stability, and social prestige. Joseph's father, Neil R., had

Joseph MacPherson

once expected much from his son; Joseph would demand nothing less from his children.

* * *

S ome might say that fate brought the MacPherson and Nicholson families to live about a half mile apart in Sydney, Cape Breton by 1918. Others would call it a coincidence. Patrick Nicholson and Annie MacPherson, as fervent Catholics, probably believed that their meeting at a dance represented the will of a very good and gracious God. No one could argue with the fact that the bond they formed through the sacrament of Matrimony was sacred and unwavering. This bond would be tested time and again, but the trials of life only strengthened their devotion to each other.

Did Patrick convince Joe MacPherson that he was a worthy suitor for Annie? Or did she simply defy the will of her father and follow her heart? In either case, Patrick and Annie exchanged wedding vows at Sacred Heart Church on October 15, 1918. This was a time when the Great War, later known as World War I, was winding down in Europe. Soldiers returning to their homes around the world carried a virulent influenza strain which was particularly lethal to those in the prime years of their lives. The resulting "Spanish Flu" pandemic wreaked havoc on communities everywhere. Sydney was no exception. Many cities enacted laws to control the spread. One regulation restricted public gatherings, so the wedding of Patrick and Annie was held very early in the morning. Only the bride and groom, their sponsors, and the priest were allowed to attend.

Afterward, the newlyweds traveled by train to Mabou, Cape Breton for their honeymoon. Family lore held that for as long as he lived, Joseph MacPherson would attempt to determine whether his daughter, Annie, was being adequately cared for by her husband.

Paddy and Annie Nicholson

Paddy took on a new role in the Nicholson household when he and Annie returned from their honeymoon. His father, Young John, had become sickly, his condition described as one of "general weakness," and he passed away on November 4, 1918, at the age of sixty-eight. His mother Maggie remained with Paddy and Annie, who helped her raise Lily, her adopted daughter, and maintain the family home on Douglas Street in

Sydney. Times were changing, but they were a family, always knowing they could rely on each other through thick and thin.

Annie was awakened by a sharp abdominal pain like nothing she had ever experienced. She reached over and clutched her husband with fear and dread.

Oh, Paddy, I think you better go find the doctor. This pain is bad. The baby may be coming, and it's too early. Annie panted through the strong contraction, relieved when the pain subsided for a few minutes. It was August 17, 1919, and the baby was not due for another month. She knew that babies born too early had little chance of survival, yet she hoped that a doctor might be able to prevent this premature delivery. As she stood up to try and get to the bathroom, she realized in panic that the baby was not going to wait for the arrival of the doctor. But Paddy was out the door and making his way to find Dr. Walsh while his mother, Maggie, rushed to Annie's side.

Please try to get back in bed now, Annie, Maggie pleaded. *Paddy will be back soon with Dr. Walsh, so try to lie back down.* Maggie fished in the pocket of her robe to find her rosary beads and silently began praying to the Blessed Virgin for a miracle.

When Dr. Walsh and Paddy finally returned, the doctor asked everyone to leave the room while he examined Mrs. Nicholson. Labor pains were coming quickly now, and it was clear that there was nothing in his kit that would stop the progression. When finally Paddy and Maggie heard a weak whimper, they rushed to Annie's bedside. Dr. Walsh looked up at the father, and his expression betrayed the dread that he felt. The baby girl was so tiny and pale; barely a movement could be detected as the doctor held the limp child in the palm of his hand. Paddy went to his wife and stroked her damp forehead while they both looked to the doctor for some words of encouragement. Dr. Walsh tried for what seemed an eternity to revive the tiny infant, patting her on the back, rubbing her skin, and swaddling her in a blanket for warmth. The Sacred Heart parish priest came to baptize their infant, whom they named Mary. Then he administered the last rites of the Church, as their hopes for her survival faded. Now, they prayed for her soul, and she was buried the next day, Monday, August 18.

* * *

P addy came home wearing a big smile on his face. *The Sydney steamfitters have voted to organize into the union. They'll be Local 209. It's been a long road, but all the work has finally paid off.* He beamed as he set a twenty-dollar bill down on the kitchen table. Annie looked up from her work peeling potatoes at the sink. She was finally feeling stronger in body and spirit. It had been a few months since the death of baby Mary, and she hoped the coming winter would not be as severe as the past few. She hoped that Paddy would begin to find more painting jobs now that the war was over. She hoped and prayed that the tension in the labor movement in Sydney would not place her husband at risk of injury or worse. The time had come for them to have the discussion that she had been rehearsing in her head. Drying her hands on her apron, Annie began,

> *Paddy, I know how important the unions are to you. I know how important you are for workers in Cape Breton. But I also know that we can't live on sentiment, much as we wish we could—there's just no corned beef and cabbage in it. I'm glad you were able to succeed with the steamfitters, and I know we have some good uses for that money you brought home today, with Christmas coming. But I think it's time to take your mind and your heart away from labor and unions and try to concentrate more on the painting.*

She saw his expression change as she spoke. This wasn't the first time they had broached the subject of his work. His passion for the rights of workers was unbounded. He had so little formal schooling, but he read everything he got his hands on. He had a keen understanding of the power struggle that always under-mined the legitimate claims of the working class. The work of the labor movement was natural work for him, but unless there was a more just and favorable compensation for his efforts, it would never be enough.

Paddy understood Annie's point of view, and she was right. He was now in his thirties. He was responsible for her, and now that his father was gone, his mother and Lily relied upon his support, too.

I know, Annie. I'm after doing all I can for labor. It's time to move on. I'll put an ad in the paper for painting and wallpaper hanging, and maybe some jobs will come our way.

Advertisement in Mosgladh Gaelic Magazine, vol. 1 (1), 1922, page 4.

And so by 1920, P. McE. Nicholson resigned from labor union organizing and labor newspaper reporting. Annie could now sleep a little easier knowing that her husband was not going to be at the center of the violent confrontations that oftentimes cropped up at the workplace and on the picket line.

* * *

Annie and Paddy waited with patience as they continued to pray that God, in his mercy, would bless their marriage with children. Their hopes and prayers were answered early in 1922, when on the second of February, their family grew to three with the birth of a healthy son. They named him John Joseph Nicholson, in the Gaelic tradition after both of his grandfathers, Young John Nicholson and Joseph MacPherson. In a nod to his Scottish heritage, Paddy added a second middle name, Kentigern, the patron saint of Glasgow, fondly known as St. Mungo. He was baptized by Father MacAdam on the fifth of February, with Paddy's brother Dan and Annie's sister Catherine serving as the boy's godparents. Although they didn't realize it then, the second of February would prove time and again to be a momentous day in the Nicholson household.

* * *

I am going to marry Annie Mae in August, Dan Nicholson told his brother, Paddy, just after the christening of John Joe in February 1922.

Dan, that is great news! I know you and Annie Mae will be very happy. You know we love her and her family, and we welcome her into our own, Paddy replied, as he patted his younger brother on the back. Paddy was not surprised at Dan's announcement, because Dan and Annie Mae had been seeing each other lately. Annie Mae lived with her father Michael N. MacNeil and his second wife Elizabeth (MacKinnon) along with Annie's six younger siblings. Paddy could well imagine how tough it must have been for them all after the death of Annie Mae's mother in 1917. As the eldest daughter, it became her responsibility, at just sixteen years of age, to help raise the little ones after her mother died in childbirth. Annie Mae had to drop out of school so she could take on all the responsibilities of motherhood for six little ones ranging in age from two to thirteen. She was twelve years younger than her fiancé, but she was ready to start a new life as Mrs. Daniel Nicholson.[5]

The couple married on August 8, 1922. Their first child was born on June 14, 1923. Paddy and Annie Nicholson were godparents for Margaret Anne at Sacred Heart Church in Sydney. Three months later, Dan and Annie Mae returned the favor as they became godparents for Paddy and Annie's second child, Mary Sarah Nicholson, born on September 6, 1923. Named in honor of her grandmother, Sarah MacNeil, she was called Sadie by family and friends, and later in life, she was known to her nieces and nephews as Sister Sadie after entering religious life in the community of the sisters of Notre Dame du Namur.

* * *

Father Patrick J. Nicholson returned to Nova Scotia after his ordination in 1916. He was ready to begin a distinguished career of teaching and administration at St. F. X. University. He developed a reputation as an outstanding scientist and professor of physics and was well known on campus by his nickname, Doc Pat. "He served over the years in many administrative and other capacities as well. At various times he was Registrar, Dean, Spiritual director and Choir Director in addition to his regular duties as Professor of Physics."[6] Indeed, Doc Pat was instrumental in molding St. F.X.

into the acclaimed Catholic university it had aspired to in 1905 at the time of its fiftieth anniversary.

On top of his academic work, Doc Pat took on the additional responsibility of writing and editing a weekly column in *The Casket*, a newspaper published in Antigonish. He was a passionate advocate for Gaelic language and culture, and his column, entitled "Achadh Nan Gàidheal" allowed him to "preserve the Gaelic language and his beloved Scottish heritage."[7] Years later, that column became the vehicle through which he and his cousin Paddy collaborated to share the folklore and oral traditions of their home—the Loon Lake country of Rear Beaver Cove.

Chapter 13

To the Boston States

Goodbye, my son. She stepped up to him and kissed him upon the forehead. . . . The son, an upright, lithe, well-favored boy, looked at her a little wistfully as if the tone and manner of her farewell had left a tremor of disappointment in his soul: but he caught her to his heart in a sudden boyish embrace, impressed a warm kiss upon her cheek, and without a word turned from her and was gone.

— A Man in Overalls, 1918

P addy's mother Maggie understood all too well that worry was a constant emotion for many mothers and grandmothers. Fretting about events beyond their control couldn't change them. Still, she was unable to manage her anxiety whenever her loved ones were involved. Now, in the fall of 1924, her sons were separated by hundreds of miles for the first time in their lives, even living in different countries. What thoughts consumed her mind? What would become of her family?

It's been almost a whole year since Dan and Annie Mae left Sydney. They've been good to write, but it just isn't the same. Until last October, Dan was never far from home. Everything seemed okay when he was here. He could laugh like no one else, so loud and so strong. You'd have to smile whenever he was in the room. And that baby, Margaret Anne, was so sweet and tiny. When they told me her name would be Margaret, the tears just rolled down my cheeks. There was not a whimper from her when we waved goodbye to Annie Mae, cradling tiny Margaret at the train station. It was so hard to send them off, but we shouldn't have to worry about their safety anymore. With all the troubles around here, I sometimes wonder if I'll ever see them again!

During the Great War, everyone prayed for peace and prosperity. Warring countries finally signed the armistice and ended the fighting exactly one week after my husband John died. Then, our mourning gave way to thanksgiving and great hope for better times. That hope faded before too long, and instead, we've seen conditions gradually worsen for nearly everyone around here. It's already been six years of world peace, but there's little of that in this part of Cape Breton.

You can't blame the returning soldiers for expecting to come home and find good jobs in the mines and at the blast furnace. Instead, many companies that made products for wartime are now closed. Sydney is dependent upon the steelworks, but instead of hiring more steelworkers, the plant has laid off many of its longtime employees. On top of that, they evicted the workers' families from their company houses, throwing their possessions out onto the street. Paddy said that the steelworkers have been unable to form a union that would be recognized by the company, so they are on their own. Even the government has failed to come to their aid. It seems the *provincial government is often more sympathetic to the company than to workers and their families.*

Thank God Annie was able to talk sense into Paddy. She understood how devoted he was to the labor cause, but she's a very practical woman. Four years ago in 1920, even before John Joe was born, she had to let Paddy know that they couldn't get by on the wages of a union organizer. She always said, "There's no corn beef and cabbage in it," and she was right. If anyone could convince him, it was Annie. So Paddy left the labor movement, and yet the labor movement never really left Paddy. I suppose there's not a person living in this area who has not been affected by the strikes that have only worsened every year since 1920.[1]

When the coal miners' pay was cut by a third in '22, they walked out of the pits and took the maintenance workers with them. Without maintenance workers, there was no one to run the equipment that keeps water and gas from seeping into the mines. Fortunately, the strike ended in ten days, but not before provincial troops were called in to help company police protect the power station and keep the mines from flooding. Had that happened, it could have permanently destroyed the mines. Then, there'd be no coal or steel industry at all.

Last year, the steelworkers walked out for higher wages and recognition of their union by the company; instead, the company ordered their police along with troops from Halifax to maintain peace in the area. I'll never forget what happened on Sunday, July 1st. We heard about it from our neighbors and read the accounts in the paper. It happened at the very time that people were getting out of church, walking home along the city streets. Police and troops, many of them on horseback, rode through town and attacked innocent bystanders with their batons. Young and old alike were struck down, injured by the officers who were sworn to protect the public from harm. It was

*said a great number of the troops were intoxicated during the
ruckus.*

*After that incident, coal miners voted to join the steel-
workers on strike, demanding that the use of military force in
industrial disputes must end. They would not return to the
mines until the troops were withdrawn from Sydney. By Tuesday, July 3rd, ten thousand miners had walked out. This
included the critical maintenance workers. All miners and
steelworkers were out on strike. For so many families, this
meant more misery and hunger that continued throughout the
summer of 1923. Some of the strike leaders have been arrested
and charged with "seditious utterances." I know Paddy is
starting to worry that he might become a target because of his
prior role in union activities. Some newspapers have led people
to believe that labor activists are all socialists or even commu-
nists! Paddy says that some folks even call him a devil. They
taunt him, saying he has cloven hooves. He believes he is being
watched and that there are witch hunts underway to round up
anyone with leftist leanings.*

*After last summer, hunger and desperation finally ended
the strikes at the mines and the steel plant. Yet only some of the
workers were allowed back. The companies have blacklisted a
good number of workers, calling them agitators. Paddy tried to
help the blacklisted men get back to work, and they were very
grateful to him for his efforts. Others have been forced to leave
the area, moving to western Canada or the United States,
because the steel mills and mines in Cape Breton will not hire
them back.*

*For the rest of us who've remained here in Sydney, prices
for food and everyday needs have risen to the point that so many
are barely able to feed their children. It often makes me wonder
why we ever left the Backlands. At least we could grow our food
there, hunt and trap for meat, and catch fish. When I was little,*

living with my parents, sisters, and brothers in Northside East Bay, we were never for want of a good meal. Of course, there were hard times, but we pulled together, worked hard, and had lots of fun with each other and our neighbors. We were up against Mother Nature at times, but she was more forgiving than the men who run BESCO (British Empire Steel Company). Well, I suppose it's too late to consider going back to country life. We will find a way to go forward as we have many times before. It's probably just a matter of time until Paddy and Annie decide to pack us up and move to the States with Dan and Annie. What will spark that decision? I hope we are not too late.

* * *

After a long train ride through Nova Scotia and New Brunswick, Dan Nicholson crossed the border at Vanceboro, Maine on September 26, 1923. He was excited about this trip, looking forward to seeing his friend and former coworker, Hugh MacNeil. He and Hugh had worked together on the tram lines in Sydney and Glace Bay, but Hugh left for the Boston States about four years earlier, intending to marry Florence Johnston. Now, Hugh was studying to become a nurse in Roxbury, Massachusetts. When Dan first entered the United States, he was unsure how and where he might find work as a painter. But he felt certain his opportunities would be much better south of the border. Once he found a job and a place to live, Annie Mae and Margaret Anne could join him and they would settle down. He wished his brother, Paddy, would have accompanied him, but he understood that such a life-changing decision was not one to make hastily.

It didn't take long for Dan to find exactly what he was seeking, but not in Roxbury or anywhere in the Boston area. Maybe he saw a newspaper advertisement or talked to someone he'd met on his travels. In any case, he found a job in north-central Massachusetts at a factory in Gardner. There, he could use his painting skills in the finishing department of one of the numerous chair factories in the area churning out wooden chairs and baby highchairs to be shipped to all parts of the country. Gardner and its surroundings drew a sizable number and variety of immigrants to good factory jobs in the chair industry, and the town became known as "Chair Town." Immigrants from several traditionally Catholic countries, including French Canada, Ireland, and Poland, built neighborhoods around their churches and worshipped together on Sunday mornings at Sacred Heart (Irish), St. Joseph's (Polish), and Holy Rosary (French) Catholic Church.

Could Dan Nicholson have imagined when he left Cape Breton that within one month, he would be joined by his wife and daughter? How little time it took for them to settle in and make Chair Town their new home! There, he met an Irish immigrant who had established a beverage bottling company in 1894, selling wine, beer, and liquors as well as carbonated soft drinks. Thomas Brazell, "a leading figure in Gardner's business life,"[2] was a devout Catholic, active in Sacred Heart parish and its affiliated organizations. By 1920, prohibition had become the law of the land, putting a crimp on one aspect of Brazell's bottling business. So in 1922, he purchased the E. L. Thompson Company, a chair making and finishing business located in Baldwinville, about five miles from Gardner. The chair factory would supplement his losses in the beverage industry until the time when the 18th Amendment was repealed. Brazell's son, John, became head of the company. Thomas and John Brazell got to know Dan Nicholson through the parish and offered him a good job with E. L. Thompson. The chair factory was five miles from Gardner, but Dan recognized that this was an opportunity he could not pass up. Annie and Margaret Anne arrived at the U. S. border on October 30, 1923.

How many times did Dan implore his brother to consider leaving Sydney?

Paddy, you have to come up here to Gardner. We're all worried. Even Mumma is ready to get away from all the troubles. Really, how can you stay in Sydney when you're after looking over your shoulder all the time? I wouldn't be saying this if the job was not a good one. Brazell's a good man. He came to this country the same way the rest of us did, and he worked his way up the ladder. Now he owns two businesses and he's respected in the town and the Church. I know how hard it is to leave home. I love Cape Breton as much as anyone, but the way it is with all the strikes and the police and the troops, it's just a matter of time before someone is badly hurt. Just say the word and I'll talk to Brazell and you'll be on the job with me in the finishing area. You're so good with people, they might make you the boss!

Paddy knew that Dan made a compelling argument whenever they talked about the future. There were some very good reasons to consider moving the family up to Gardner with his brother's family. He had honed his talent as a painter and was considered a master of the craft. Working in a chair factory with Dan would be a satisfying occupation, one in which he could apply some of the painting techniques that he had acquired over the years. In addition, he'd developed leadership skills while representing the Brotherhood of Painters and Decorators in the Sydney Trades and Labor Council. He might enjoy the challenge of management if that opportunity presented itself. As the weeks and months passed, and the new year of 1925 loomed on the horizon, the prospect of becoming an American became ever more appealing. Perhaps leaving Sydney would be the right move, even a matter of self-preservation.

* * *

For Annie and Paddy, 1925 began on a happy note. Their third child, a daughter, was born on the first of January. Three days later, Margaret was christened, named after her grandmother. However, good times for the Nicholsons were soon tempered by serious labor troubles. On the sixth of March, after BESCO management refused to negotiate a new contract with the UMW, 12,000 miners took to the picket lines, leaving a small crew of maintenance workers to maintain water pumping and electricity in the mines. By June, with no progress toward a settlement, the Great Strike of 1925 took a violent turn with desperate families facing the prospect of starvation. The union pulled their remaining maintenance workers out to the picket lines, and, on June 11, the company responded by sending their police to escort company workers to restore water pumping and electricity-generating stations in the mines. A confrontation between miners and police turned violent when company police fired a barrage of gunshots into the picket line. William Davis, a miner and the father of nine children, was killed when a bullet hit him in the chest. Many other strikers were injured. Following this tragic incident, striking miners looted the company stores, which were subsequently burned to the ground. The strike was settled after government intervention, but the violence of June 11 is remembered annually on Davis Day in mining communities of Nova Scotia.

Paddy had officially left the labor movement in 1920, but violence in the community impacted him and his family. He believed that he was being watched as if there was a target on his back. Perhaps his brother, Dan, was right. Yes, he concluded, it was time to leave Cape Breton, his homeland. It was time to move his family to a safer location. The riots of June helped him make up his mind. On the fourth of August, he crossed the border at Calais, Maine with forty dollars in his pocket; his destination, Gardner, Massachusetts. His border crossing paperwork showed that he was seeking work and that his brother Daniel Nicholson was his sponsor. Once in Gardner, he found a home for the family at 163 Washington Street, a few blocks from Dan and Annie Mae. Two months later, Annie and his mother, Maggie, arrived with Lily, John Joe, Sadie, and infant Margaret Genevieve. What a joyful reunion that was!

* * *

The growing town of Gardner proved to be a temporary home for the Nicholson brothers following their move from Cape Breton to the United States. Gardner had almost everything that a family would need: church, schools, and shopping. However, getting to and from work was burdensome for Paddy and Dan. The factory was five miles away. Neither of the brothers owned a car nor could they drive. So once again, they began looking for homes closer to work. As luck would have it, they soon found houses within spitting distance of the E. L. Thompson Chair Company.

The town of Templeton is composed of four villages: Templeton Center, East Templeton, Otter River, and Baldwinville. It is located in Worcester County just west of Gardner and about twenty-five miles northwest of the city of Worcester. The Otter River flows through Baldwinville and the village of Otter River, powering the numerous factories lining its banks. One of the factories was the E. L. Thompson Chair Company. It was near this factory that Paddy and Dan Nicholson purchased homes on Maple Street in Baldwinville. Paddy paid $2,400; Dan paid $1,200. They were living so close to their work in the finishing shop that they could look out the window and see their homes just across the street.

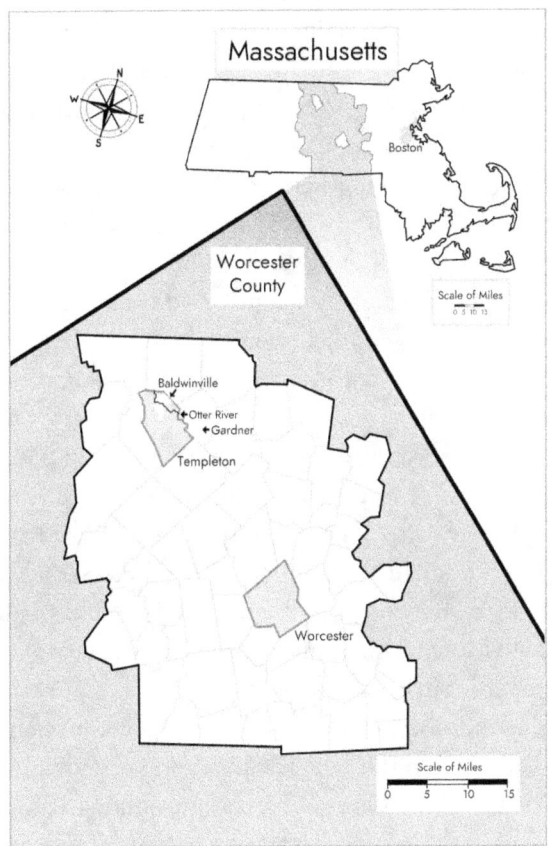

The American economy was booming. These were the Roaring Twenties. Dan and Paddy had steady paychecks and their wages were on the rise. Factory orders continued to grow and the future looked promising. Paddy became superintendent of the finishing shop, where the chairs were dipped in vats of stain at the end of the manufacturing process. Sometimes decals were added to embellish the products. The brothers embraced their new American life. Paddy filed papers on May 2, 1929, declaring his intention to become an American citizen.

The Catholic church nearest Baldwinville was St. Martin's in Otter River, about a mile and a half from the Nicholson homes. Founded in 1851, many of its earliest parishioners "traveled by foot, by horseback, and by wagon from as far away as Orange and Ashburnham to attend Mass. . . . [These were] an immigrant people seeking home and livelihood, determined to practice the faith which was their heritage, [who] endured many sacrifices and tolerated extreme hardships to practice the religion which meant so much to them."[3] Paddy and Annie Nicholson, together with Dan Nicholson and Annie Mae, continued this legacy, becoming faithful contributing members of the St. Martin's community.

A new pastor, Father James T. Reilly, arrived at the parish at about the same time as the Nicholson families. Paddy and Dan became friendly with Father Reilly and offered to paint the church in their spare time after work and on Saturdays. The pastor came to know these brothers as dependable and talented craftsmen who could be called upon as needed to keep the parish properties in good condition.

Sunday mornings were busy in the Nicholson households. Everyone dressed in their best clothes and headed out the door for the long walk to Otter River. They couldn't eat breakfast before Mass in those days, because those receiving communion were required to fast from midnight until after the service. How they wished for better transportation between their homes and the church, but buses did not run on Sundays. That gave Paddy an idea that would help the Baldwinville parishioners get to Sunday Mass on time. He approached the local bus company with a business proposition: run a bus through Baldwinville every Sunday morning and transport people to St. Martin's in Otter River in time for Mass. How much would it cost per person? Would they provide the return trip for the same rate? The proposal was well received. The fare would be five cents per person each way. The bus filled up each week and so did the pews of the church for the celebration of Sunday Mass.

All the children of both Nicholson families were required to take the bus to church every Sunday. But the older ones could decide whether to ride back or save their nickel fare for other uses. Sadie and John Joe preferred to hoof it home for a chance to buy a Mr. Goodbar on the way!

Holy days of obligation that fell on weekdays were a different story, though. All of the buses were obligated to their regular routes through the village, so there wasn't one to take them to the Church. Mass was early—7:00 a.m. On such occasions, just the older children walked the distance with Pop and their Uncle Dan.

Keep up, John Joe! said Uncle Dan. *You're getting out of step!*

Catholics Not Welcome

Hey Pop, what's that burning out in the yard? John Joe followed his father out the door and around the side of the house, where they discovered a large cross set afire on their property. The message was clear. A burning cross was the signature of the Ku Klux Klan. Why would the Klan target the home of Paddy Nicholson? John Joe helped his father put out the fire and together they tore down the charred remains. This was not the first time the Klan had made its presence known in Templeton and surrounding communities.

Throughout American history, there have been separate and distinct periods of Klan activity, each having the purpose of achieving a *purification* of American society. The first appearance of the Klan after the Civil War in 1865 was confined to the Southern states and focused on issues related to race and Reconstruction. The organization was dissolved in 1871 after failing to achieve its goals. The second Klan began organizing in the early 1920s, intent on growing its membership throughout the country. They expanded their objectives and tactics to achieve the overarching goals of purifying politics, strict morality, and enforcement of Prohibition. They considered certain groups of people, including Jews, Catholics, Blacks, and immigrants, a threat to society. They organized parades, like one held in Gardner in late April 1925, to bring attention to themselves and their message. They wanted people to know that the Klan was active in their community.

FLAMING CROSS AROUSES PEOPLE OF OTTER RIVER

OTTER RIVER, Feb 18—A flaming cross, on the Otter River Board Company dam, early this morning, aroused excitement in the town. Selectman Percy C. Young had the cross torn down and thrown into the river. The dam where the cross stood is within a few hundred yards of St Martin's Catholic Church.

The Boston Globe, February 19, 1925, page 15.

A few months before Paddy arrived in Gardner, the Boston Globe reported that a burning cross had been found in the village of Otter River. The location of the cross, "within a few hundred yards of St. Martin's Catholic Church," was seen as a warning to the clergy and parishioners of that church— Catholics were a threat to society and, as such, targets of Klan activity in the area. Paddy had drawn attention to himself as a public figure in the Catholic community after he arranged Sunday bus transportation to Mass at St. Martin's Catholic Church in Otter River. By helping fellow parishioners get to church on Sundays, he became the target of the local KKK. But it wasn't long before the second wave of the KKK, like the earlier version, was flattened and left to smolder for decades until the time of the American Civil Rights movement in the 1950s and '60s. Yet the vision of that fiery cross remained fixed in the memory of young John Joe, who, like his father, made sure the written and oral history of the twentieth-century Nicholson clan would not be forgotten.[4]

* * *

Many more Nicholson children were born in Baldwinville between the years 1926 and 1937, filling up the homes of Dan and Paddy. Dan and Annie Mae had four boys: Michael, John, Martin, and Daniel. Their cousins referred to them by their traditional Gaelic nicknames: Mickey Uncle Dan, Johnny Uncle Dan, Marty Uncle Dan, and Donny Uncle Dan. A daughter, Mary Patricia, born on March 31, 1930, died less than two weeks later.

My grandparents had five more children in Baldwinville: Donald Thomas, Catherine Rhodena (Dena), Anna Mae (Anne Marie), Mary Patricia, and James Anthony (Jimmy). Jimmy was named in honor of their pastor, Father James Reilly. An infant, born after Jimmy died in childbirth. That night, their father faced the anxious older children with the announcement, "Jimmy will always be our youngest child." His oldest brother, John Joe, never forgot that moment nor the sadness he saw in his father's eyes.

My mother, Anne Marie, nicknamed Anna-Ree, was born in December 1929, a few weeks after Black Tuesday—October 29, 1929. Her childhood years were marked by the austerity of the Great Depression. Hard times impacted her, her family, their community, and many others throughout the country.

Maggie Nicholson (top center) with Paddy, Annie, and children, at their home in Baldwinville.

The Radio

Every day, the local newspaper was delivered to the front door with news of the region and the world. Sports scores, financial reports, and schedules for upcoming events and entertainment were reason enough that every household subscribed to the paper. The classified ads gave everyday folks a way to find a job, buy or rent a home, and purchase all kinds of new and used goods, from furniture to firewood to pets. Local stores and businesses paid for large columns to advertise their products and any special sales they were having. Readers pored over the ads to find deals on all the latest inventions and products that could make life easier and more enjoyable.

By Christmastime in 1925, radio programs were being broadcast to those fortunate enough to have a radio to receive them. That year, the radio was advertised as "A Gift The Entire Family Will Enjoy." There was something for everyone on the radio, including music, sporting events, and variety shows. For as little as two dollars a week, baseball fans could hear the

PUT CHRISTMAS JOY INTO YOUR HOME!

A Gift The Entire Family Will Enjoy

Superfine New 'Pearson' Radio Outfit

$89.00

Advertisement in the Fitchburg Sentinel on December 17, 1925, page 9.

play-by-play action of their favorite teams and experience the World Series games as they happened. A little money down, easy weekly payments, and professional installation made owning a radio a high priority. Within a decade, over sixty percent of American households had a radio.

Did you see this ad in the paper this morning, Annie? asked Paddy.

Annie had looked over the newspaper this morning and was pretty sure she knew which advertisement her husband meant.

What ad would that be, Paddy? He knew that Annie was anything but frivolous with money. She could stretch a dollar farther than anyone he had ever known. So he thought carefully about how to broach the subject with her.

Wouldn't it be great to have a radio of our own, Annie? I think the payments would be affordable after the raise I got last month. Out of the twenty-five dollars we get every week, the radio will set us back just two. You can listen to the afternoon serial shows, and Amos 'n' Andy is on every night at seven. Won't the kids love that, too?

Annie was receptive to the idea. *Well, Paddy, I think you've set your mind to it already. I do believe we can make the payments if the store or the bank will lend us the money. We'll find a way to make ends meet, we always have. Seems everyone in the neighborhood is coming home with a radio these days. Why don't you go to the store and talk to them about their easy terms?*

So like so many of their coworkers and neighbors, the Nicholson family became the proud owners of an Atwater Kent Radio set. Buying on credit was a concept unfamiliar to these Cape Breton natives, but their world was changing fast. They realized that if they had to save up for major purchases those purchases would never materialize. There was always something that would get in the way of their desires. Ever since they arrived in the U. S., opportunities for a better life seemed to crop up regularly. The American economy was thriving, and you would know all about it if you read the local paper. Their income was rising, so they were feeling the prosperity that they expected to find in America. Right now, there was no reason to believe that these good times would ever end.

Once the radio was installed, they found they could receive broadcasts from as far away as Boston, New York, Washington, Pittsburg, Philadelphia, and beyond. Sports, variety and comedy shows, the news, and every type of music—jazz, blues, swing, and ragtime—could be enjoyed just by turning the dial. In addition to Boston Red Sox and New York Yankees baseball, boxing was a strong draw in those days. Paddy loved boxing, so they probably listened to the broadcast of the world heavyweight championship on September 22, 1927, between Jack Dempsey and Gene Tunney. Two weeks later, the World Series began on the afternoon of October 5, and the New York Yankees won in four straight games over the Pittsburgh Pirates. Though Paddy was at work during all of those games, he was just across the street from home. Annie was instructed to listen to the games and hang a red cloth on the clothesline anytime the Yankees scored a run. In this way, Paddy was able to *hear* the World Series and keep up with the action as it happened. Oh, what a grand investment that Atwater Kent radio was![5]

When the good, strong economy of the 1920s gave way to the Great Depression, many workers were laid off from their jobs. The stock market tumbled and people stormed the banks to withdraw their life savings as they began to fear that the stability of the banking system was collapsing. Luckily, Paddy's job at the chair factory was secure, but for many workers, paychecks were slashed. Between 1929 and 1931, the average hourly pay for a finisher at a furniture factory fell by 20 percent, from 51.5¢ to 41.4¢. Many who had purchased household items "on time" found themselves behind in their payments. Such was the case for Paddy and Annie Nicholson and their beloved Atwater Kent radio.

* * *

D*addy, Daddy, I was just up at Uncle Paddy's house, and a man came in to take away the radio. He was so mean and told them to give it back to the store or go to jail!* said Margaret Ann breathlessly as she stormed into the living room. That was all Dan needed to hear. He raced out of the house and up the street to his brother's house, just in time to see the finance company man disconnect the radio from the wall socket. Paddy was trying to convince the repo man that it would just be a few more days until he received his check from the factory.

What in the world are you doing? Dan demanded, snatching the electrical cord from the grasp of the man. *Who do you think you are? You can't take that away from my brother. He owns that radio.*

Straightening up, the two men were eye to eye and chest to

chest. *I am Gardner Higgins from M.A.C. Finance. This radio needs to be returned today, and I'm here to take it myself.*

Gardner W. Higgins had found himself in this position many times. His job was not an easy or pleasant one. Perhaps he had been hired by the M.A.C. Finance Company because of his strength, his youth, and his experience as a strongman. He had learned to expect the possibility of confrontation whenever he paid a call on customers who had failed to make the agreed payments. It was more the rule than the exception. Who wouldn't protest? Nevertheless, an agreement was an agreement, and these were contracts, signed and sealed. Until the owner's brother had entered the room, it seemed that this time, tempers would not boil over. Now, it was clear that was not going to be the case.

Your brother hasn't kept his side of the bargain, and I need to take back the radio until the payments are up to date, declared Higgins in a calm voice. But he had a smirk on his face that seemed to show a certain enjoyment, a superiority over these delinquents. That was all Dan needed to see. Blocking the front door, he reached out for the radio. He had never felt so angry and he would let this man know it. *Over my dead body,* he shouted. Then he took a swing, which luckily missed its mark. Higgins put the radio down momentarily as he roughly shoved Dan aside and once again lifted the heavy box and lugged it out of the room toward his automobile, parked at the curb.

All the hollering had attracted the attention of neighbors, who feared that the repo man may cause some real injury to either Paddy or Dan. Soon the town constable showed up, and Higgins complained that he had been assaulted by the brothers. *Now wait,* Paddy said as calmly as he could manage. *If any assault occurred, it was you who entered my home and forcibly took my radio. Then you pushed my brother who was just standing in the doorway.*

We'll have to let the judge settle this, gentlemen. You'll both receive a summons to appear in court so be prepared to state your cases. Fill out this form and you will hear directly from the clerk as to when to appear, stated the officer.

That settled it, for now, and Higgins left with their Atwater Kent.

The court date was set for Thursday, July 25, 1930. Patrick had to get excused from work to go to First District Court to plead his case. Dressed in his best Sunday suit, he walked into the courtroom as the mild-mannered, humble man that he usually was. His prior work with the labor movement in Glace Bay and Sydney had prepared him for such an appearance. Calm and collected—that was the attitude he needed to display this afternoon. His brother Dan, always the more excitable, was similarly contrite as he followed his brother up to their assigned seats. When called to the bench, they again met the finance man, Gardner W. Higgins. Mr. Higgins reiterated his assertion that he had been assaulted by the Nicholson brothers when he was merely trying to repossess the radio. It was his job. Nicholson was behind by several weekly payments.

After hearing both sides of the issue, the judge determined that the assault had not happened as described by Higgins, and those charges were dismissed. Instead, Higgins was fined $15 for his heavy-handed behavior in taking the radio from the Nicholson home. After providing all the delinquent payments to get the radio returned, the case was settled.

> Gardner W. Higgins of Fitchburg, an agent of the M. A. C. Co., a finance corporation, was fined $15 for assault and battery in first district court yesterday afternoon. Higgins was charged with attempting to take a radio from the home of Patrick Nicholson, Baldwinville, on which, it was alleged, payments had not been kept up. Nicholson objected and the two men exchanged blows. Higgins swore out a complaint charging Nicholson with assault and battery, but he was discharged.

Fitchburg Sentinel, July 26, 1930, page 7, column 1.

That night, the family gathered to enjoy the seven o'clock broadcast of *Amos 'n' Andy*. For the Nicholson children, the pleasure and trouble brought to the family by the Atwater Kent radio would be hard to forget.

Hard Times

The Great Depression of the 1930s left few communities in the U. S. or Canada untouched by severe economic uncertainty. Those who were able to work were lucky. Some companies went out of business, and many large ones were forced to lay off portions of their workforce. The E. L. Thompson Chair Company continued to manufacture good quality chairs, and Paddy and Dan Nicholson were fortunate enough to remain employed as chair finishers. Nonetheless, their growing families learned to live within their means. There was nothing to spare above and beyond the bare necessities of food and shelter.

Winter days were short in Baldwinville. Around Christmas, the sun rose about 7:15 in the morning and set as early as 4:15 in the afternoon. Electricity to run household appliances and lights was costly, and Paddy's family tried to conserve as much as possible. How often it happened that Annie would be preparing supper, or the children would be trying to do homework and suddenly the lights would go out! This would set off a desperate scramble for a coin. *See if there's a quarter in the bureau, John Joe.* He'd fumble around in the dark and, if lucky, locate the necessary coin. Then he carried it to the cellar and dropped it into the electric meter. The lights would come back on, and the radio would resume broadcasting the evening's programs. That would get them through the night, but what would they use tomorrow?

How many times did Friday come around with no cash left in the drawer until the next payday? Whenever Annie discovered this dilemma, she'd write a quick note requesting an advance on next week's pay. *John Joe, take this note to the company office.* The boy returned with a few dollars, and the family would be spared the embarrassment of having no money for the Sunday offertory collection. Annie would find something they could do without that week, something she could scratch off her grocery list. Vegetable barley soup goes a long way.

An Omen

Maggie Nicholson felt lucky to be living with her sons and their families in the United States. She got news regularly in letters from relatives and friends back in Cape Breton and she sensed that life there was much more difficult than hers in Baldwinville. She enjoyed being around the children, and her presence in the home was a blessing for Annie, Patrick, and the children. She helped Annie take care of the youngsters, prepare meals, wash clothes, and clean the house. She was getting older now, but, at age seventy-four, she felt strong and fit. She had adjusted to life in this small American town over the past five years. She lacked for nothing. But if asked, she would have to admit to missing friends and relatives with whom she had grown up in East Bay. And there were those neighbors from Rear Beaver Cove, Glace Bay, and Sydney that she would often think about and pray for at night before she slipped into her bed.

Of course, the Nicholsons of Baldwinville were not the only Cape Breton natives living in Massachusetts. For decades, waves of immigration brought young workers from Canada seeking opportunities in the States. Johnny Gillis was a friend who lived with his family on the outskirts of Boston. Maggie was excited to have a chance to visit with them for a few days in September 1931.

Annie and the children sat outside the front door to watch for Johnny's car while Maggie finished packing her suitcase. The kids were anxious to meet these folks, these Boston people, but John Joe was concerned about his grandmother traveling all that way. He loved his Nana, a kind and gentle woman, and he worried for her safety on such a long trip. He went into her room while she was folding her sweater and held out a little round tin.

Here, Nana. I got this for you so you can take it with you on your trip. He knew that his grandmother occasionally enjoyed a bit of Garrett snuff, and he had saved up his pennies to get some for her. Maggie just smiled and thanked him as she placed the tin into her bag.

I'll be very careful, John Joe. You don't have to worry about me. Johnny Gillis is a good man and a good friend of my family. Maybe you can go visit them sometime. Now your school year is just starting, and I hope you'll study hard and learn a lot this year. If you do, you could become a priest someday. You would be a wonderful and holy priest! John Joe grinned at his grandmother as she said these words. He had sometimes thought about this and knew how proud his parents would be if he ever became a priest. He practiced saying Mass and he knew all of the prayers in Latin and English. Yes, he wanted to make them proud someday.

He followed his grandmother out into the front room, just as a little bird flew through the open front door and landed across the room on the window sill. The children started yelling and running around, trying to coax the little bird out of the house. Maggie slowly walked to the window and gently pulled up on the sash, giving the visitor an easy escape route from all the commotion. But did her calm expression hide the alarm that she might have felt knowing the old Scottish myth: A bird in the house foretells a death in the house?

A few days after Maggie left with Johnny Gillis for a visit to Jamaica Plain, Paddy received word that his mother had been involved in a terrible accident in that city. It was Thursday,

September 3rd. The next day would be First Friday, a holy day revered by many observant Catholics. Maggie had just been to confession at All Saint's Church in preparation for First Friday Mass. Paddy read the message to Annie, his voice choked with emotion. *She was struck by a car as she crossed the street by the church. The driver of the car took her to the hospital. I'll go tell Dan now. We have to get to the hospital in Boston, fast.*

Annie grabbed the chair for support as she listened with disbelief to the words her husband was speaking. *It was the bird! The bird was in the house before she left,* she thought. *Oh, Paddy, I can't believe what I'm hearing. Oh, please, dear God, watch over Nana and give her strength.* But Paddy was already out the door and headed to his brother's home to make the necessary arrangements to get to their mother's side.

> **WOMAN SERIOUSLY HURT**
> **BY CAR IN JAMAICA PLAIN**
> Mrs Margaret Nicholson, 64, a widow of Baldwinsville, is in a critical condition at the Boston City Hospital with a probable fracture of the skull and minor injuries sustained last night by an automobile at Centre and Highland sts, Jamaica Plain.
> The automobile was operated by Herbert A. Fenton of 92 Rockland st, West Roxbury, who took Mrs Nicholson to the hospital.

The Boston Globe, Friday, September 4, 1931, page 2, column 5.

When they reached the hospital, the two men were escorted to a small waiting area. Soon after their arrival, the doctor who had treated their mother came into the room.

Are you Mrs. Nicholson's sons? he asked Paddy and Dan. *Your mother suffered a fractured skull and a broken pelvis when she was struck by a car. They rushed her to the hospital, but I am very sorry to have to tell you that she has succumbed to her*

151

injuries. I also want you to know that we did everything in our power to save her life. I'm so very sorry.

This was the news that Paddy and Dan had dreaded as they traveled to Boston that evening.[6]

The pastor of All Saint's Church in Jamaica Plain entered the waiting room just as the doctor was leaving. He approached Paddy and Dan, shaking hands with each of them as he introduced himself. He spoke slowly and softly, with sincerity and respect. *I was devastated to learn of the tragic accident that took the life of your mother. I only met her yesterday in the confessional, but I can say with confidence that she was a holy and God-fearing woman. She is enjoying the bliss of her heavenly reward at this very moment. I hope that will be some consolation to you and your loved ones.*

Thank you, Father, they mumbled in unison.

The priest continued, *Johnny Gillis and his family considered your mother as close to themselves as anyone. They share in your grief.*

Paddy nodded and replied, *We are going to Johnny's after we leave here. They are lifelong friends, as close as any kin. We want them to know that we have no ill feelings toward them. They will help us find a way to take our mother's body back to Baldwinville.*

Maggie Nicholson's casket returned with her sons to Otter River for a funeral Mass at St. Martin's Church. Then, Paddy took John Joe with him to the train station to make arrangements for the return of his mother's remains to Sydney, Nova Scotia where she would be laid to rest beside her husband in Holy Cross Cemetery. The agent prepared the paperwork, stamped it firmly, and pushed it across the counter for Paddy's signature. The words OF NO VALUE in large, black letters overshadowed every other word on that form. John Joe watched as tears of sorrow fell from his father's eyes. His dad scribbled "P. McE. Nicholson" across the bottom of the form because of the necessity to do so, but without affirmation. Those three words went against everything John Joe had ever learned about human dignity, in life and death. Yet here it was stated that his beloved Nana, the wonderful lady who lived with him since the day he was born, was now someone of no value.

* * *

By the time John Joe finished eighth grade at the Baldwinville public elementary school in 1936, he had seven younger siblings. Economic conditions in Baldwinville and everywhere else continued to deteriorate as the Great Depression left many people jobless and hopeless. Paddy's pay barely kept up with the expense of feeding, clothing, and sheltering the large family, but it was more than many others had. It was around this time that something completely unexpected happened.

Father James T. Reilly had been pastor of St. Martin's Church in Otter River for nearly the entire time that the Nicholson families lived in Baldwinville. During those years, Father Reilly got to know Paddy and Dan very well. Their families attended Mass faithfully every Sunday and Holy Day. They donated to the collection. They offered their time and talent to help the pastor maintain the parish buildings, church, and rectory. They even painted the church when it was needed.

In 1933, as was customary in those times, Father Reilly was transferred to Holy Rosary Church in Spencer, Massachusetts, a small town about twenty-five miles south of Otter River. After just three years at Holy Rosary, Father Reilly learned that he would again be reassigned, this time to a large church in nearby Worcester. The Church of the Ascension was a growing parish, located on Vernon Hill, a community of Irish immigrants. As pastor of Ascension, Father Reilly was responsible not only for the sacramental life of his parishioners but also for the care and maintenance of the church grounds. There was a rectory for priests, a convent for the nuns, a high school, and an elementary school. Because of the size and complexity of the parish, Father Reilly's move to Ascension entailed substantially more responsibility than he had in his previous assignments. He was going to need a conscientious caretaker for the routine maintenance of all five buildings, keeping them clean, clearing walkways and parking areas after snowstorms, stoking all of the boilers with coal every morning, and attending to problems that developed now and then. Yes, he knew that he would need someone he could trust to care for the physical needs of this parish just as diligently as he cared for the people's spiritual needs. He needed a strong, dependable, and devout Catholic man for this job and he knew just the man. How could he convince Paddy Nicholson to uproot his family during this economic depression and move to Worcester? Knowing Paddy as he did, Father Reilly was sure that there was one factor that would tip the balance in favor of Worcester—something they would have in Worcester that was not available in Baldwinville.

* * *

Paddy came home from work one evening with an expression of bewilderment on his face. It was a look that Annie had seen time and again over the years of their marriage. Gone was his usual lighthearted and carefree demeanor, which seemed to be ever-present despite the hard times. Indeed, she knew him well and she sensed that he had something important on his mind.

Paddy's faith in God was enough to keep him optimistic and

hopeful, satisfied with his lot in life, and confident that his family's needs would be met through hard work and prayer. As the sole breadwinner for the family, he was well aware of his financial responsibility for the children's wellbeing. At the same time, he counted on his wife to make his paycheck stretch to the limit in running the home and keeping the family on budget. She was the practical one, the financial wizard. She knew how to maximize a dollar's purchasing power. Together, Paddy and Annie Nicholson shared the belief that children should be as well-nourished in mind and soul as they were in body. Their priorities were that each of their eight children would grow up strong in their Catholic faith. Everything else would work out as long as this one goal was achieved.

Paddy motioned to Annie that he wanted to speak to her privately in a corner of the room. There they huddled, as he explained the matter that had consumed his thoughts that afternoon. Most of the children paid no attention as their folks were locked in a most serious conversation. But John Joe could see that whatever they were discussing would impact their lives one way or another. He would soon learn that he was correct.

How long ago it was that Paddy's uncle George uprooted his family from their home in Rear Beaver Cove so that his son, Patrick J. Nicholson, could get a solid, fundamental education in North Sydney. That education would prepare him for admission to the university in Antigonish. Yes, it was over thirty years ago, but Paddy remembered vividly the day his cousin Pat moved away from Rear Beaver Cove. He recalled his own mixed emotions—pride for his cousin while at the same time, disappointment that his own educational opportunities were over. Moving to North Sydney as a boy allowed Pat to graduate from St. F. X. with a BA degree in 1909. From there, he went on to a doctoral program in Physics at Johns Hopkins University in Baltimore. One achievement after another led Doc Pat to the seminary, and by 1916, he was ordained to the priesthood at the age of twenty-nine. He was now Father Patrick J. Nicholson. What honor he brought to his family and the Nicholson name.

Baldwinville had small public schools, but as Father Reilly explained, St. John's Catholic High School was a short walk from Ascension Church. Students who graduate from St. John's go on to study and earn degrees from colleges like Holy Cross and Boston College. Father Reilly himself had graduated from Holy Cross before entering the seminary.

> *I believe it would be a great opportunity for John Joe. Isn't he about to start high school? I'd like you to come to Worcester and work for me at Ascension parish. I know the quality of your work, Paddy. I think your family would benefit in so many ways if you would consider this proposal. The girls can go to Ascension School from first through twelfth grade. After grammar school at Ascension, the boys will go to St. John's for high school.*

Explaining Father Reilly's proposal to Annie, it became impossible for him to disguise his excitement at the possibilities. Annie knew then and there that the move to Worcester was going to become a reality. *Where would we live?* she asked, and Paddy had all the answers.

> *The parish owns a three-decker next door to the rectory. We would live on the bottom floor. It's right next to the church. We wouldn't need to take a bus to church or work or school. We could walk wherever we need to go. What do you think, Mumma? Should I say "yes?" Can we make this move for the sake of the children going to good, Catholic schools? Perhaps one day a "Father Nicholson" will come from our family.*

156

Annie began to feel the excitement herself. They would have to move soon because the new school year would start right after Labor Day. She would miss Dan and Annie-Uncle-Dan, as they called her sister-in-law, but they could visit each other, since Worcester was not but twenty miles from Baldwinville.

It had been over ten years since they boarded that train in Sydney to move to a new country. That move hadn't been so bad. Moving into the big city of Worcester would likely have some benefits for her and the children above and beyond the church and school. Perhaps food would be more plentiful in the stores near their home. What new conveniences might their home have? There was not much time to dwell on the decision. If this was something Paddy thought would be best for the family, who was she to think otherwise? *Go ahead and let Father Reilly know we will be coming,* Annie said. *Tell Dan, too. We can explain this to the children at supper tonight.*

With that, the family packed up all of their meager possessions. Paddy talked to the man who delivered chairs for the E. L. Thompson company. He agreed to help the family move into their new home. They loaded up his truck with their furnishings. Paddy, Annie, and all but one of the children rode in the cab. *There's no more room here, John Joe. You'll have to ride in the back of the truck. Hold on tight and don't let anything fall out!*

Okay, Pop, John hollered, gripping the side of the truck bed with all his might. As they pulled away from their home in Baldwinville, Paddy waved goodbye to his brother one more time. He was probably heartened by knowing that his children would have opportunities the likes of which he had always craved. Even when the inevitable difficulties of life surfaced in Worcester, Paddy, and Annie never doubted that this was the best decision they could have made and they thanked God for opening this door for them.

Chapter 14

Worcester

What . . . carried my mind's eye both into the future and the past was two large cranes flying slowly straight and sure, south by west across my vision, going to their winter home. Where did they come from? Some Bylot Island in Baffin Bay. How often have they traveled the same unchartered trail?. . . Did they rest at Loons Lake and see the country of my Tales?. . . When I was a youngster did they travel the same path, after I am no more will they still carry on? Perhaps . . . when we are no more, when this is a better world, when all is united in the brotherhood of man under the Fatherhood of God, descendants of these same birds will cross the vision of some dreamer like myself, . . . traveling still the same unchartered course, their bills ever forward, sure of themselves and of where they are going.

— P. McE. Nicholson, 1943

Annie Nicholson was always a woman of few words, never one to complain. But for those who knew her well, there was seldom any doubt about her opinions or her feelings. And so from the first moment that she stepped across the threshold of their new home in Worcester, her husband Paddy recognized her disappointment. Though the home they left in Baldwinville was no castle, there had been plenty of room for everyone, all ten of them. Now they'd be as crowded as sardines in a tin can, living in five rooms on the first floor of a Worcester three-decker.

The three-decker had become an icon for the city of Worcester. Three identical flats were stacked one on top of the other, each with a couple of bedrooms, a kitchen, a dining room, and a living room. Three-deckers sprung up in working-class neighborhoods of the growing city during the late nineteenth and early twentieth centuries, as manufacturing and milling industries expanded and the population grew. Many families residing in these units were recent immigrants from Ireland, Italy, Poland, Sweden, or Greece, working in Worcester's textile mills, wire and machinery factories, shops, and markets. Ethnic communities developed, centered around churches and schools that served the spiritual and educational needs of their immigrant families.

Paddy Nicholson was to be the custodian for the Ascension Parish, and in that capacity, his family was provided one apartment in the three-decker behind the church on Dorchester Street. The upper two floors were already occupied, so the Nicholson family would live on the first level. Two bedrooms would have to suffice for this family of ten until someone residing above them moved out. On the positive side, the children could walk to school and Paddy could walk to work, which was a big advantage since he did not drive a car and was always at Father Reilly's beck and call.

The two bedrooms were side by side off the kitchen. The girls—Sadie, Margaret, Dena, Anna-Ree, and Mary—slept in the back bedroom. Annie and Paddy slept in the other bedroom with baby Jimmy in his crib. The older boys, John Joe and

Donald, slept on the couch in the living room, or "front room," as it was called. They all shared one bathroom. It was tight, but they would make do. Paddy believed firmly that their sacrifice would be worthwhile because the children would be able to attend parochial schools. Their lessons would be taught by the Sisters of Notre Dame, who lived in the convent next to the church. Students received a firm grounding in the basics of reading, writing, and arithmetic as well as the fundamentals of their Catholic faith. There was reason for optimism; the economy began improving as the decade of the thirties wound down. Only time would tell what the forties would have in store for them.

The boys were permitted to attend the small school at Ascension through third grade, but beginning in fourth grade and throughout high school, they'd have to walk down Vernon Street to Saint John's School on Temple Street. At fourteen, John Joe's first year of school in Worcester was his freshman year of high school. After graduation in 1940, he enrolled as a day student at Holy Cross College, planning to take a pre-medical course of studies leading to a Bachelor of Science degree. When Father Reilly heard this, he took the young man aside to give him some advice. *Why don't you work toward a Bachelor of Arts, John Joe? Take courses in theology, philosophy, Latin, and history in addition to the science courses you might need for medical school. Although you think you will become a doctor someday, the Lord may have other ideas in mind for you. You must keep your heart open and be ready to answer the call if you receive one.* His words did not fall on deaf ears.

* * *

Father Reilly proved to be a demanding boss for Paddy. He had been ordained to the priesthood in 1905, then assigned to missionary duties in Cleveland, Ohio for two years, after which he "traveled the country as a missionary, preaching in 48 states and Canada."[1] Could this have explained his rough manner in dealing with people under his authority?

We need to prepare to paint the exterior of the church this summer, Father Reilly barked as Paddy entered his office on the first floor of the rectory that Monday. *It won't be an easy job, but I don't think it's been done in many years, so I want you to begin making the arrangements.*

Isn't that so, Father, answered Paddy. *We should take care of Our Lord's house better than we do our own. John Joe will be off school for the summer; he will be a big help.*

Paddy had been wondering when he would be called upon to start this epic undertaking. The church had a high facade; no ladder would get them up to the highest point. Paddy would visit the paint shop to get an idea of how much paint they would need and speak to the proprietor for suggestions on how to tackle such a daunting endeavor.

When John Joe returned from his classes that afternoon, his father was waiting for him on the front porch. *I've got a job in mind for you this summer. We're going to paint the church. We'll start as soon as you finish your exams.*

Sounds great, Pop. John Joe enjoyed spending time with his dad, for whom he had tremendous respect and fondness. Being the eldest of this large family, he was given a great deal of responsibility. Oftentimes he felt that Pop relied on him not only for help keeping up the parish properties but, maybe even more importantly, for advice and guidance. It was a good feeling. He was beginning to see that he was at his best when called upon to help folks who needed it. *Isn't that what doctors do?* he thought to himself. *Or maybe . . .*

Paddy and John Joe started preparing the church for painting by scraping off the peeling paint and sanding the shingles within their reach. That phase went smoothly, and it was about time to start applying the paint. However, the problem of working at the height of the church caused both of them a good deal of anxiety. They did not have the proper equipment so they would have to improvise. Paddy had an idea. *We can lash our two longest extension ladders together with rope. That might get us within reach.*

Once the ladders were tied together, they leaned the contraption up against the front of the church. John Joe did not expect to hear the next of Pop's ideas. *Go on up there now, John. I'll hold the ladder for you.* So the young man, trying to hide the dread and fear that caused him to break out into a cold sweat, ascended slowly, rung by rung. But his pace changed abruptly once he reached the top. He slapped on that paint in broad, rapid strokes, eager to get back down to the safety of solid ground. Then and there, John Joe ruled out any future occupation that would require a ladder.

* * *

After the attack on Pearl Harbor in December 1941, President Roosevelt declared war on Japan. A few days later, America was drawn into the war in Europe. By the first days of 1942, the government informed citizens about some of their wartime responsibilities. One of the first civil defense procedures to be implemented was the use of blackouts. "The purpose of blackouts is to deprive enemy airmen of all possible reference points which might aid them in locating definite targets." Blackouts would require "painstaking planning and advance preparation as well as full cooperation from the people at large. . . . The responsibility for execution of blackout procedures rests with the chief warden."[2] Every night, citizens were required to remain in their homes, put out lights in any rooms that could not be effectively blacked out with curtains, and refrain from using matches or lights outside.

At the age of fifty-five, Paddy was fully committed to the war effort and sought some way to contribute as best he could. The duty of a local blackout warden might be something he could take on for his neighborhood. He was a well-known and highly respected citizen of the community; in fact, he was the ideal man for the job. He was conscientious in his duties and fulfilled his responsibilities faithfully.

As John Joe was completing his second year at Holy Cross, he registered for the selective service, or the draft as it was commonly known, just as every other young man born between January 1, 1922 and June 30, 1924. However, because he was a full-time college student, he was deferred from active military service at that time. He was a member of the class of 1944, but because so many soldiers were needed, his class was put on the fast track to early graduation. Instead of having a summer break in May of 1943, the men were required to continue their coursework through the summer between their third and fourth years. They finished the first semester of their last year and began the second semester after a brief break. Come Christmas-time in 1943, John Joe received his BA from Holy Cross College.

He applied and was initially excited to learn he was accepted to medical school at Georgetown University in Washington, D.C. Wasn't this why he had worked so hard throughout college? Certainly, he had wanted to become a doctor ever since his first biology class at Holy Cross in the fall of 1940. Wasn't medicine the ultimate career for a person who wished to help others, cure the sick, and care for those in pain? But the advice Father Reilly gave him before he started college kept nagging at him. Was medicine his calling? Or did God have another plan for him, another path that he could take to reach his goal of helping people and caring for those in need? After serious thought and counseling from his spiritual advisor, John Joe concluded that he was being called to the church, to the priest-hood. When he told his parents of this realization, they could not have been more pleased and proud. Their response assured him that he had chosen the right path.

Paddy just looked at Annie, and she knew what he was thinking: that their decision to move to Worcester back in 1936 had been the right one. It was the best move that they could have ever made. Memories flooded back to Paddy of the time forty years ago when his Uncle George packed up his household and moved from Rear Beaver Cove to North Sydney so that his son, Patrick J. Nicholson, could attend school. And look how far that education had gotten his cousin in those forty years. He was now "Doc Pat," with a doctorate in Physics, and he was an ordained priest. News had just arrived from Antigonish, Nova Scotia that Doc Pat would become President of St. Francis Xavier University in September 1944! Paddy was proud of his cousin for all his achievements. He was thrilled to think that John Joe, his son, would soon enter the seminary. The good God works in truly remarkable ways!

* * *

One day in the winter of 1945, Paddy Nicholson fell sick with the grippe. Of course, living in such close quarters, the whole family soon developed symp-toms of the flu and they were all confined to bed for the week. It was unusual for Paddy to be out of work, but it could not be helped. Hopefully, none of them would get pneumonia. Rest was needed to get them back on their feet.

After about a week, Paddy began feeling much better and decided it was time to get back to work. Heading out to check on the convent, he stopped in the rectory to pick up his pay envelope. When it wasn't in the usual location, he knocked on Father Reilly's office door. Entering the room, Paddy asked, *Have you forgotten something, Father?*

What do you mean, Paddy? Father Reilly replied without looking up from his paperwork.

I don't see my pay envelope on the table, Father.

The priest put his pen down and glared at the man standing before him. *You haven't worked all week!*

The terse response stopped Paddy in his tracks. A million thoughts ran through his mind. Father Reilly knew there were little ones at home. The family needed that income. They lived from paycheck to paycheck with no extra money to put away for times like this. He had never taken a sick day before this. How was he going to tell Annie that there would be no money coming in until next week?

Paddy tried to think of something to say to make Father Reilly change his mind. Knowing the man as he did, though, there was probably nothing short of turning back the hands of time that would remedy this situation. So, not wanting to make matters worse, Paddy turned around and retreated without saying another word. He would not plead his case. What could he do?

That evening, when Paddy returned home without his pay, he told Annie the grim news. *I'm not getting paid for last week, Annie.* She could hardly believe what he was telling her. They had a family to feed and bills to pay, and they had to put their envelope in the collection basket on Sunday. She looked at her husband, so humble and forsaken at that moment. She wanted to tell him it would be okay, that they could make do, but her reply seemed to come from somewhere deep inside her, expressing the true despair that she was feeling at that moment.

What are we going to do, Paddy? In her mind, she was calculating how she could stretch the food in their pantry to last another week. How could their pastor have acted with such indifference to their needs? He knew they had a large family. With the salary that Paddy received, there was never any money left over at the end of the week. They had no savings, no rainy day fund.

I'll go to the bank, Annie. Perhaps they can help us out this one time.

If this had been the first time that Father Reilly had oppressed his janitor, Paddy might have dismissed it. Maybe Father was just having a bad day. But over the years, the man seemed to find it ever easier to take advantage of Paddy's good nature and his desire to please his employer. He was a priest, after all, and priests were the representatives of Jesus. The priest should always be given the benefit of the doubt. However, it was becoming clear to Paddy that Father Reilly had become very disrespectful and short-tempered with him. He had always been a faithful servant. No, he certainly could not accept the way he was being treated. Withholding his pay after a week of sickness was the final straw for Paddy. He had to do something about it.

The next day, he knocked on Father Reilly's office door once again. *Who's there?* came the curt reply. Paddy probably said a little prayer for courage as he opened the door and walked into the room. Taking off his hat, Paddy stated firmly, *I've come to hand in my resignation, Father. I am done.*

This got Father Reilly's attention. He looked directly into Paddy's eyes and without a shred of hesitation, stated in no uncertain terms, *Are you sure you want to quit?*

Paddy never wavered in his determination to leave the job. *With all due respect, Father, I can't continue to work here under these conditions.*

Don't you have a son in the seminary? Things could get very difficult for him.

Father Reilly might just as well have punched him in the gut and knocked the wind right out of him! Paddy couldn't believe his ears, but the threatening tone of voice made the message crystal clear. He was unprepared to hear those words from this man, who had once given him such hope for his family's educational opportunities. Father Reilly had called his bluff.

There was no way Paddy would ever do anything to put his son's future as a Catholic priest in jeopardy. Father Reilly had all the cards, and they both knew it. *I'll get back to work now, Father, and perhaps one day we will forget we ever had this conversation.*

Father James Reilly passed away the following year, on May 13, 1946. The new pastor immediately awarded Paddy Nicholson a substantial pay raise.

John Joe completed his studies at the Grand Seminary in Montreal in January 1948. He was ordained at Saint Michael's Cathedral in Springfield, Massachusetts, and celebrated his first Mass at Ascension Church in Worcester on January 25, 1948. Family and friends from near and far came to share the joy of this day with Paddy and Annie Nicholson and their son, whom they would now call Father John Joe.

* * *

A Man in Overalls

Reverend John J. Nicholson blesses his parents after his
ordination in 1948.

P addy Nicholson had left Cape Breton for the United
States in 1925. The Nicholson family made a good life
in Massachusetts. As soon as he was able to do so,
Paddy became a naturalized American citizen. He took seriously the duties and responsibilities of citizenship. But in many
ways, he never forsook his homeland. He never forgot his ancestors. Over time, thoughts of Rear Beaver Cove—The Big Glen—
crept into his consciousness more often. He found himself
dwelling on memories of the old folks who were so important to
him when he was young. Watching his children grow up in
Baldwinville and Worcester reminded him of how starkly
different his childhood had been. *Oh, if only they could have
known his Granny! What stories she told him about Barra and
their journey to Nova Scotia! Of all the people he had known in
his life, it was she who impacted his character more than any
other.* "The mystic curiosity that grew in me I owe to her. . . .
She knew more lovely Gaelic prayers, more songs, stories and

folklore than anyone else I ever knew."[3] So he began to write about what he remembered.

The beauty of the terrain surrounding the Bras d'Or Lakes remained vivid in his mind as well. The stories of Cape Breton remained alive in him. Yes, now he was just a janitor but he had been a writer. Once a writer, always a writer! So he began to write, and his stories burst out like a wildflower bloom on a late spring afternoon.

* * *

W*hat are you doing, Daddy? It's very late!*

Anna-Ree, I should be asking you what you are doing! replied her father as he glanced up from his writing. *Don't you have school tomorrow? What do you need?*

I was thirsty, Daddy. I saw the light on in the kitchen. Can you get me a drink of water? pleaded the ten-year-old curly-haired girl.

Of course, I will. Let me just finish one thing first, he replied as he scratched out a few more of his thoughts onto the paper before him. After handing the child a glass of water, he patted the seat of the chair next to himself at the table. She sat down and looked over at the stack of papers spread out in front of her father on the old wooden table.

What is it that you are writing, Daddy? A letter to someone? Her father was always writing or reading something after he finished his workday.

No, Dear, right now I'm working on a story.

Oh, I love stories, Daddy. Can you tell me the story? Who is it about? Sister Mary Teresa is always telling us stories about the saints in school. Is your story about one of the saints? Her father was beginning to think that he should have sent her right back to bed after her sip of water, because she might have trouble getting back to sleep and then trouble waking up in the morning.

Not tonight, Dear. I promise I'll tell you all about it once I'm finished. The story I'm writing was told to me by my grand-mother many years ago. She knew so many stories, and songs and prayers, too. I was so lucky to hear her tell those stories, and I want you and the others to be able to read about our family and learn about where they came from. But right now, you must run along back to your bed. Morning will be here before you know it, and you need your beauty rest.

After Anna-Ree had gone back to bed, the house settled into a perfect peace. This was the time of day that Paddy cherished. It was the one time that there were no other demands on his attention. The needs of the parish could wait until sunrise. The sounds of modern-day household chores were silenced. Even the muffled sounds of traffic out on Vernon Street could be ignored. Looking out the window, he paused for a moment to appreciate how the full moon drenched their small yard in a silvery glow. It was the quiet, peaceful serenity, together with the natural light of the night, that brought his mind back to a time so long ago and a place so far away: the Loon Lake country that he named "The Big Glen."

* * *

The dictionary defines folklore as "The traditional beliefs, customs, and stories of a community, passed through the generations by word of mouth." The stories that Paddy's grandmother, Catherine MacMullin Nicholson, brought with her from Barra to Cape Breton were rich in these qualities. Scenes were set within the familiar communities where she lived with her kin, complete with vivid descriptions of the surroundings and the individuals. The characters were legendary. Mystical, indeed miraculous occurrences were common themes, and the truth behind the events was never doubted by the listeners.

In a 1923 essay in the Dalhousie Review, Beatrice M. Hay Shaw noted:

> There is only one way of collecting genuine folklore, and that is to obtain it directly from the people who have themselves received it in the same manner from those who preceded them. . . . The older people are often shy of telling these stories to strangers for fear of ridicule. The younger generations are half inclined to ridicule them themselves. Thus, as years go by, a great deal of folklore disappears in every country. There is no shadow of doubt that those who are interested in preserving all the records and history of the Maritime provinces should lose no time in making a concerted effort to form a genuine collection of stories.[4]

It was thinking like this that propelled Paddy Nicholson to embark on a project to turn the oral history of his family—captured in his youth and stored for decades in the vault of his memory—into a written collection of Cape Breton folklore. Fortunately, his efforts forestalled the prophecy of Beatrice M. Hay Shaw, namely that

> A large portion of the data will undoubtedly be lost forever, as the generation that retains intact the old traditional tales . . . is dying out under the iron-shod heel of modernity and progress.[5]

* * *

When Paddy and Annie emigrated to the States in 1925, they left behind in Canada several close family members. Had they wished to visit them during the twenty years between their arrival and 1945, it probably would have been nearly impossible. Their children were young, money was scarce during the Great Depression, and wartime travel restrictions in the early 1940s limited in-person visits to just the most essential. They would have relied on the mail to keep each other up-to-date on all the news, happy and sad alike.

Annie corresponded with two sisters and a brother living in Sydney. Her sister Catherine had married Alex Campbell of Red Islands, and they had five children. Her youngest sister Mary Anne was married to Reggie Martin of Sydney; they had one son. Annie's brother Neil MacPherson was married to Jennie Gillis, and they had two sons.

Paddy also maintained contact with some of his kin back in Canada. His brother Alexander, who had spent time working in Miami, Florida, settled in Windsor, Ontario by 1935, the year that his wife Margaret passed away. They had five children. Paddy's sister Jessie and her husband Malcolm MacDonald raised a family of six in Glace Bay.

* * *

By 1940, around the time when Canada joined Britain in the fight to halt the aggression of Hitler in Europe and before the United States was drawn into the war, P. McE. Nicholson and his cousin Father Patrick J. Nicholson were hatching a plan to ensure the survival of Nicholson family folklore. Both men were determined to preserve and protect the language, traditions, and culture of their Gaelic ancestors. They were now in their fifties, living hundreds of miles apart in different countries, but somehow, they recognized that they had a limited opportunity to accomplish their shared goal. Father Pat had taken on a great deal of responsibility at St. F. X., and on top of that, he was writing a weekly Gaelic column in the Antigonish weekly newspaper, *The Casket*. Paddy had begun writing folklore stories based on the lives of his grandparents and other inhabitants of Rear Beaver Cove, The Big Glen. He didn't write in Gaelic, so he sent his stories to Doc Pat to translate them into Gaelic and published them in his Gaelic newspaper column. The cousins found an appreciative and captive audience of readers who "had the Gaelic." Together they would preserve their heritage.

"Your story is positively tremendous," Doc Pat wrote to Paddy in June 1941.[6] Nothing in the world could have cheered or encouraged Paddy more than seeing those words on paper. He believed this story was good, and God knows he loved every minute spent working on it, but to get such praise from his well-respected, highly-educated cousin was more exciting for him than he could have imagined.

"As you may well understand, not a few things were difficult to express [in Gaelic]," wrote Doc Pat. "I take it that the tale is based on fact."[7] To avoid any confusion on the matter of the factual basis of his work, Paddy marked his manuscript as "The first in a series of *true* stories from the Loon Lake region, by P. McE. Nicholson."

The next letter from Doc Pat arrived in late July. "I intend getting your story into print within a few weeks. . . . My great desire is to get as much as I can of worth-while songs and tales in type before everything is forgotten. The literature I am chiefly interested in is the old folk tale."

ACHADH NAN GAIDHEAL

AN RATHAD FADA

Le Padruig Iain Alasdair

3

Mu dha uair 's a' mhadulnn, rainig Micheal an Gobhal aig bonn Beinn Mhic Gille-Moire far an robh lorg a'

as mo dheidh dol thairis air an ait' fhosgailte, agus chi mi 'n sin e." Gun dail, ghabh e air aghaidh gus an run seo a chuir an gniomh.

Dh' fheith e gu samhach fad dheich mionaidean am fasgadh nan craobhan seilich 's e 'g amharc air

"The Long Road" by Padruig Iain Alasdair published in Gaelic in the Casket, 1941. Courtesy of St. F. X. Archives.

"An Rathad Fada" (The Long Road) appeared in print in the fall of 1941. The author was identified in the Gaelic tradition by his *sloinneadh* (patronymic), Padruig Iain Alasdair (Patrick John Alexander).

This was a heartwarming tale of a man whose journey was interrupted by a mysterious force that ultimately saved his life. The story was well received by the Gaelic community of Cape Breton. In November, Paddy received a letter from his "good old friend" J. J. MacInnis from Sydney. "Ever since I read your excellent story in *The Casket* a few weeks ago, I had a desire to contact you and compliment you highly on this very interesting story, and the excellence of the language used. I have been in touch with the works of Gaelic writers, both in Scotland, and in this country more or less the past thirty-five years, and I find your production, "Gabh an rathad fada glan," second to none with the best of them. My good friend, come again with more. The Prince of the Gaels, Father P. J. [Nicholson, Doc Pat] will be pleased to assist you."[8]

Did such an encouraging message compel Paddy to continue writing his stories of folklore, sending them to Doc Pat for translation and publication in *The Casket*? In a letter dated March 22, 1942, Paddy received a response from his cousin regarding "Just Off the Trail," conveying welcome praise. "Believe me, it is no mean effort, and those to whom I read it were deeply impressed." This is a story of two neighbors in the Backlands who walk miles through heavy snow to the chapel to have their spring seed blessed before the planting. A folktale of faith and the power of humility, it would have brought hope and simple joy into the homes of a war-weary populace.

More stories followed "Just Off the Trail," and after each, Paddy received kind and encouraging letters from Doc Pat. "It is quite a little while since I received a charming tale from you, written in your usual excellent style." (July 18, 1943) Coming from Doc Pat, those words brought great satisfaction to Paddy. Despite their vastly different backgrounds and educational experiences, he and Doc Pat worked well together. They shared the overwhelming desire to ensure that Gaelic folklore, first heard at the knees of their grandparents, would not be lost forever.

Was it the scientist in him that compelled Doc Pat to confer with other family members about some of the more mysterious happenings in the stories? Most often, he found confirmation from one of the "old stock." But once, Doc Pat was not able to establish the veracity of the events in Paddy's story. In his letter of July 18, 1943, he wrote,

Dear Patrick,

I did not feel like proceeding with the translation right away because I couldn't feel assured of the accuracy of your facts. Since that time I visited Cape Breton and made inquiries. The legend of the light might indeed be known to very few: the death of an infant uncle of ours within a few years of the arrival of the grandparents would be known to many, I would suppose. Anyhow, I checked on that, and my two sisters, your own sister, and . . . Ronald Gillis of Boulardarie all state that no infant son of theirs had died. . . . And so, much to my regret, I cannot publish the tale except as a bit of fiction, with fictitious names. Anyhow, I shall be glad to hear what you have to say about it when you get a chance. . . .

Yours faithfully,
Patrick George

The story in question was titled, "The Hill They Blessed." Paddy set the story in the early time after his grandparents sailed from Barra and began to settle Cape Breton. They faced monumental hurdles, not the least of which were fierce winter storms. Through their trials, they experienced events that could only be seen as supernatural. Such is the foundation of a good deal of Gaelic folklore.

Paddy's inspiration for the story came about because of his close bond with his paternal grandmother, Catherine MacMullin Nicholson. He explains this to Doc Pat, writing "I believe I can say without exaggeration that I knew my grandmother better and lived closer to her during the last ten or so years of her life than anyone else. In fact, she was more of a mother and a teacher to me than anything else." The passion of Paddy's reply to Doc Pat seems to erupt from a deep conviction that his grandmother's account of her past may not have been known by many, but because of his close relationship with her, he was privy to this intensely personal information. He relays to his cousin several details that he remembered of his Granny, concluding that:

This is all a short prelude to the following facts, and my rights to acclaim them: 1) A child was indeed born to my grandparents shortly after coming to America who died in infancy. His name was William, called after his father's oldest brother. 2)

176

The remains of this little child were buried at Beavers Cove. 3) According to a very interesting conversation I heard one night between Little Stephen and Michael Donald Ban, the McKinnon grave plot was discussed minutely . . . and 4) My Grandfather was guided in a blinding snowstorm after losing his way between Boularderie and Beaver Cove by an unaccountable light and the first place he made out was the graveyard in question.

Paddy concludes this testimony by writing, "Still, he was not the first nor the last to be guided on sea and land by some supernatural sign unaccountable for by mortals."[9] The words of Jesus were perhaps on his mind, though not on the paper: "Oh ye of little faith!" (Matthew 8:26)

Whether or not Doc Pat accepted Paddy's explanation and published "The Hill They Blessed" as written, I do not know. Nevertheless, they worked together to preserve the traditional Gaelic folklore of Cape Breton, and in so doing were magnificently successful. They had been born within two months of each other in the Backlands of Cape Breton and lived their childhood years together in Rear Beaver Cove; thereafter, they went in completely different directions. Yet they came together in their later years to produce and disseminate folklore that reflected what they cherished most: their Gaelic culture and heritage. They both knew in their hearts that the stories had to be preserved for future generations. Their labor of love continues to bear fruit.

In September 1944, Father Patrick J. Nicholson was chosen to lead St. Francis Xavier University as President-Rector.

Reverend Patrick J. "Doc Pat" Nicholson. Courtesy of St.
F.X. Archives.

For ten years, he guided the institution as it grew to accommodate the great influx of veterans returning from World War II. The student body nearly doubled during his tenure as president, and he oversaw a building boom on campus. A fine physical science building, one in which I took many lectures and labs in the early 1970s, was completed during his term. He was appointed by Pope Pius XII as Domestic Prelate in 1946, giving him the title of Monsignor, and in 1955 he was elevated to Prothonotary Apostolic. He brought recognition and respect to his institution. He was "a person who lives always so close to God."[10]

The relationship between Doc Pat and Paddy didn't end when the last bit of folklore was published in *The Casket*. They continued their correspondence throughout Doc Pat's years as St. F. X. President. When he visited Massachusetts, he made a point to call upon Paddy. In June 1952, Father John Joe drove his parents and two of his sisters to Nova Scotia where they attended an ordination at St. Ninian's Cathedral in Antigonish. Doc Pat made arrangements for Paddy and Father John Joe to stay in campus lodging and booked a room at the Chestnut Lodge for the ladies. Upon their return home on June 22, 1952, Paddy wrote to his distinguished cousin with emotion that betrayed the warmth of their relationship, one that lasted throughout their lifetimes:[11]

Dear Father Pat,

You are wonderful, and you made us feel wonderful and humbly proud too. Proud of your high standards in the University and the educational world. Proud of the plucky, deep-rooted religious and sound economic program of the University you are president of and its solid and wise stand in a world going chaos. Proud that the good God has endowed you with wisdom blended with humility, with strength blended with gentleness, with purity blended with manliness, with charity blended with sacrifice—all that the good God meant to make this life worthwhile and meaningful. I could go on and on and on . . . but I shall put my thoughts in one simple phrase, "you are a 'Nicholson' and a darn good guy."

Thanks a million for everything, and we pray that the good God continues to shower His blessings on you always.

Sincerely,
Patrick Nicholson

Chapter 15

Leaving a Legacy

Ah, there goes the chattering of an old man again. Memories that are dear, that no one can take from us. Memories that are pure and good and clean, that are worth more than money or position or fame. Memories that have a touch of God's smile within them. Just the shadows of a humble life that would never hurt a human being knowingly.

— P. McE. Nicholson, 1963

Paddy and Annie's children were grown and settled into lives of their own by 1960. Father John Joe was a priest in the Diocese of Springfield, Massachusetts. Sadie, now Sister Sadie, had joined the order of the Sisters of Notre Dame de Namur, the same nuns who had taught her at Ascension School. Those who would marry had done so by the early sixties. A new generation was emerging, descendants of Paddy and Annie, Young John and Maggie, and Big Alex and Catherine. Our grandparents welcomed each of us with unconditional love and joy.

From Paddy Nicholson to his son, Father John Joe Nicholson, dated
July 10, 1963.

Paddy cherished the memories of his life, playing them over
in his mind with a certain satisfaction. Perhaps he was becoming
more aware of the years slipping past. Now, instead of writing
more folklore, he wrote letters to his loved ones, especially those
living away, too far for regular visits. For a man who didn't own
a car, couldn't drive one, even western Massachusetts or
Connecticut was too far. In a letter he sent to Father John Joe,
dated July 10, 1963, he mused:

> Yet the fall or eve of man is not too bad. We stop planning. We
> stop the ambitious dreaming of the future and instead we go
> back to memories of the past. I go back to the days of Leo XIII,
> of Cardinal Gibbons, of Queen Victoria, of Sir John Thomp-
> son, and Sir Wilfred Laurier. Back to 1907 when I left home in
> the Back Lands. When in 1909 I entered into the Labor move-
> ment and for the next 14 years gave it (the Labor Movement) all
> my energies and enthusiasm and whatever I had to give. I know
> I left my mark on the history of Nova Scotia during that time. I

was called a socialist, a fanatic, a dreamer, a meddler, an ignoramus. The Kingmaker in politics but all in all I had lots of fun and never lost my humor or a hearty laugh along the trail. We came to this country (USA) mostly to earn a living for myself and our growing family because one cannot feed young bellies on sentiments alone. But we left a trail in Cape Breton that was good and most unselfish. We also left a trail in Baldwinville for God and the Church and those are little things that one thinks of as the shadows of evenings life are lengthening. I believe wherever we are God had a place for us in this universe like a master chess player moving us here and there according to his will for our own good and for His greater glory I truly believe. Whether we are rich or poor, ignorant or learned, in the seats of the mighty or the hovel of the poor God has an important place for us if we try and do His will. Sometimes we stop in wonder and ask ourselves 'What is God's will?' We want to do it but wonder if we are. That never bothers me. God will have His will, He will bring it about whether we like it or not and the wise man will often pause and pray and ask God to direct him.

During this period, when my grandfather was in his mid-seventies, he and my grandmother made a few trips back to Cape Breton to visit relatives and friends. Sometimes they were accompanied by Paddy's brother Dan and his wife Annie Mae, who visited their son John, a professor at Xavier College in Sydney.[1] As a sociologist, John studied the development, preservation, and changes in communities established by his ancestors in the Backlands of Cape Breton—communities like Rear Beaver Cove. He had a keen interest in preserving a record of the lives of the older inhabitants of the island. Using the available technology of the 1960s, he recorded oral histories with Cape Breton natives, descendants of the Gaelic Scottish pioneers of the nineteenth century. My grandfather participated in several of these interviews, and recordings of these conversations were archived at the Beaton Institute in what is now known as Cape Breton University in Sydney.[2]

One of the recording sessions was devoted to my grandfather's personal experiences in the Labor Movement in Cape Breton between 1909 and 1920. In addition to his nephew John, other participants included Mr. Owen Carrigan, Professor of History at Xavier College, Father Brooks Campbell of Xavier College and Father John Capstick from the Extension Department of St. F. X. The tape begins with Paddy narrating his observations and activities in the movement, first in Glace Bay and later in Sydney. He speaks about attending the national convention of the Trades and Labor Congress in Ottawa and his observation of miners evicted from their company houses. He describes his interactions with political figures and their attempts to influence his reporting by offering a job paying a relatively high salary. He answers detailed questions, and at the end of the tape, one of the participants notes that, "In general, the dates and the occasions mentioned by Mr. Nicholson check accurately with Mr. Saunders work."[3]

Another recorded session involved a conversation about life in Rear Beaver Cove around the turn of the twentieth century. Present for that recording were my grandfather, his brother Dan, their cousin Roddie F. Nicholson, and Hector MacLean, the husband of their cousin Catherine Monica Nicholson.[4] Hearing the stories, the banter, and the laughter on the recording, I can easily imagine the joy those memories gave them that afternoon in 1965. In their own minds, they meandered the paths between their homes and those of their neighbors. They talked about a community of over forty families, naming each one, often in Gaelic, because to them, perhaps, those individuals didn't have an English name. Indeed, their memories were formed in Gaelic and remained so for all the many intervening years.

* * *

F ollowing his term as President-Rector of St. F. X. University in March 1954, Monsignor Patrick J. Nicholson was assigned as pastor of Saint Joseph's parish in Sydney. According to his biographical sketch,[5] he was elevated to Prothonotary Apostolic in June 1955. He returned to St. F. X. in March 1961, where he died on November 4, 1965. He was remembered as an authority in Celtic lore, having maintained his Gaelic column in the *Casket* for twenty-five years. He was the recipient of seven honorary doctorates between 1950 and 1957. His obituary in the University's *Contemporary—Alumni News* spoke of him as "the living symbol of St. F. X.... mourned by literally thousands of alumni. How remarkable that one man could so impress his mark on an institution that he and it become as one. Doc Pat was that kind of man, and St. F. X. would never have been the same without him."[6]

* * *

I n September 1967, Paddy received a letter from Sister Margaret Beaton of Xavier College. Sister Beaton worked in the college library and recognized that "many documents of historical and literary significance to Cape Breton Island were being lost due to neglect and the lack of an appropriate repository."[7] In 1966, she had begun a full-time effort to collect, preserve, and organize material of great interest to the people of Cape Breton. She called the archives "Cape Bretoniana," and her work led to the establishment of what is now known as the Beaton Institute. Sister Beaton requested from Paddy copies of his folklore about the Loon Lake country for the archives.

Dear Mr. Nicholson,

My heart has been overflowing with happiness ever since I received your 'Folklore.'. . . I am very grateful for the stories you sent me from the wonderful world of Cape Breton folklore, stories that are locked in the memories of few like yourself. Tales, such as you have sent keep us from losing our heritage in today's materialistic civilization. There is great richness in folklore worth preserving. If you and I and a few others do not bother about it, it will be lost forever. . . . Congratulations on your nice style. You have a facile pen. I really enjoyed reading every word of the stories you sent. They will be placed in your Collection—next to Dr. P. J. Nicholson. Wouldn't he be happy (with a big laugh) to have your Collection next to his own.[8]

* * *

Patrick McE. Nicholson, A Man in Overalls, passed away on July 7, 1972. In the months leading up to that day, he knew that the end was in sight. His last written work was a farewell letter to his wife and children, dated June 12, 1972, less than a month before his death. Always the bard, he began with a poem, in which he described how nature marked his passing.

I thought I would pass away before
But yet alive I am
And in all the shrubby trees around
I hear the chirping of the wrens.

A Man in Overalls

How sadly I remember, bleak morning of
   New Year
To die before the gentle violets come
And now - - 'the rose is here.'

Paddy's last months brought more than his fair share of pain and "real hardship indeed." He was no stranger to the curse of severe pain, having previously endured trigeminal neuralgia, or tic douloureux as it was known to him. Patients with this condition experience sudden, stabbing intense pain usually on one side of the face. It affected Paddy on his right side. How often Annie found him sitting at the kitchen table, cradling his face in the palm of his hand as if he could lessen the terrible throbbing by holding his jaw like a fragile robin's egg.

After years of suffering, he was willing to try any procedure that might help rid him of this curse. Father Craven, an associate pastor at Ascension parish, knew of a chiropractor in Pittsfield, a town in western Massachusetts. Father John Joe was stationed at a parish in Springfield at the time, so Paddy planned to take the train from Worcester to Springfield. There, his son would pick him up, and they would drive the fifty-or-so miles to the clinic in Pittsfield. But when the train from Worcester arrived at the station, Pop was nowhere to be seen! After searching high and low, Father John Joe was stunned to find he had overlooked his father on the platform. The pain had so transformed his appearance that he missed him entirely. Paddy may have gotten some relief from the chiropractic manipulation, but not until he underwent a surgical procedure was he finally able to escape that pain.

During the final months of his life, my grandfather experienced a new malady, the pain of cancer which settled in his spine. In his final letter to his family, we hear the voice of a man waiting, indeed longing for respite from the long-suffering hours. "I may surprise you when I say that this has been the happiest winter I ever spent in my whole life." Were his words intended to comfort those of us who were soon to grieve the loss of this gentle man? Was he letting us know that the joy he found looking back over his life helped cut through his mortal suffering just as surely as the strong medications his doctor had prescribed?

Then he describes the scene from a cherished memory, one unmistakably similar to the ceilidh of his youth. His family is gathered in the front room for a holiday celebration. Father John Joe is setting up to say Mass, converting the kitchen table into a "beautiful altar" with "linen . . . as white and clean, candles as bright, vessels as sparkling as anything in the Lateran Church, the head Church of Christendom." As everyone takes their place, sitting on chairs or the floor, he places himself "back in a corner out of the way," just like his grandfather, Big Alex, once did. Looking over his loved ones, he takes comfort in the realization that "one day we are all going beyond here. I may not be the first to leave, I surely will not be the last, but I am going to watch closely as we go home, and I will be watching closely to see if we are all going to be there, and if after ages anyone is missing, I do not think heaven would be the same to me." He makes a deal with God that "all my pains be directed toward grace for any dark lamb of our flock who may have to struggle for something that was easy for the rest of us to obtain." He was cheering for the underdog right to the end.

And then he leaves us with his notion of what truly matters in life. He writes:

> In my judgment, Joseph, the carpenter of Nazareth, was the greatest man God ever created outside of His Own Son. . . . He gave Joseph two virtues, deep humility and an absolute trust in the faith that God gave him. . . . [Joseph] never wore

the purple tunic of Israel or of Rome, but the homespun of a crude peasant. So what if there was sawdust in his beard or shavings in his hair, or deep furrows in his calloused hands? He died with his head in the lap of Mary, the Mother of God, his hand in the warm clasp of Jesus, the Second Person of the Blessed Trinity. So it is with us, let us be what God wants us to be. To hear the word of God, to believe in it, and to accept it.

Patrick McE. Nicholson wore the clothes of the crude peasant, not the flowing clerical robes of the learned Monsignor. Instead, he was the painter with paint spatter in his hair, the janitor with coal dust on his overalls and dirt under his fingernails. None of that concerned this Man in Overalls. Humility and trust, born from steadfast faith in God, were his guiding principles. And yet, with less than a third-grade education, he left his mark on Cape Breton and on those of us who knew him. Perhaps his words will continue to resonate with generations of his descendants including those yet to come, who will surely seek meaning in a very different world.

* * *

Annie MacPherson Nicholson died on the last day of January 1993. She and Paddy are buried in St. John's Cemetery in Worcester, Massachusetts.

Part Two

The Folktales and Poems of A Man in Overalls

[O]ral traditions are dynamic, communal creations, evolving over time and shaped by all those who share them . . . Through their work, writers are able to shed light on the internal dynamics that move and shape a people, but tradition bearers are capable of the same. Indeed, cultural insiders, even those with little formal education, are often remarkably capable of providing great insight into the societies of which they are part.

— Shamus Y. MacDonald, 2017

Chapter 1

The Hill They Blessed

P. McE. Nicholson

y grandfather, Big Alexander John Patrick was lost completely and he admitted it to himself with a pang of fear. It was not the first time he was lost, for, many a time he had lost the sense of direction for a moment along the bays and coves and straits between the Mull of Kentile in the Irish Sea and John of Grote's Point in the North Sea. But there he was much at home. Winds and currents, the sound of the sea breaking on rock or sand, depth of water or shriek of bird, color and thickness of seaweed were all marks that pointed direction to this hardy Barra-man as would the finest compass and chart to the modern navigator. But that night Big Alexander was on unfamiliar grounds. He was in a blinding snow storm on thin ice somewhere between the Big Island and Boisdale. It was only three miles across from shore to shore as the crow flies, but when Big Alexander realized that he was lost, he also realized that the Narrows Stream was to open to the harbor only a mile and a half west of where he took to the ice and the Barrachois Gut was open only two miles east of him. Coming across old foot marks he had made earlier in the night he realized without panic, but with real fear, that he was only walking in a circle and that each step he would take from now on may be leading him to thin ice and death. Perhaps he was too near it already and death by drowning was a constant dread among Hebrides Islanders. To make matters worse and tiring his strength and courage, he was carrying two bushels of wheat in a bag on his back — wheat, which meant food and food was scarce, most precious and hard to get in those early days of New Albin.

When the Scottish Islanders settled along the shores of Cape Breton, above all, they were land thirsty. Living on small narrow crofts, bound and chatteled by laws and limits all their lives, when they came to a new land, enormous in its vast size, free to their possession they took such large proportions that later emigrants had to take less favorable grounds or move inland to the "Rears." Big Alexander, while only a few years behind the first settlers in Cape Breton, had to possess for himself and family of "rear land." He settled in The Big Glen with many of his former Barra-men and it was a happy choice as The Big Glen proved to be a fertile, fruitful valley, beautiful beyond description in its wild rugged scenery. Here nestled in the heart of lofty mountains, warding off bitter winds and blights, lakes and rivers teeming with salmon and trout, countless streams and springs babbling constantly over cregs and waterfalls; forests of spruce and pine, of birch and maple, studded with dogwood and wild cherry, spanning as far as the eye could see into the mists and clouds of the mountain tops was the Big Glen—this was indeed a paradise to the true Scot. Here the sun shone warmly, the Spring came early, the birds sung sweetly. These Islanders were happy—happy in the communion of bountiful, if stubborn nature, in the wealth of song and stories of their past and in the firm and up-lifting faith given to their ancestors direct by St. Calamn Gillie of nearby Iona.

But the early years of their lives in the new world were years of hardship and poverty, of hard labor and constant struggle, of heartache and backache. Hunger was not only their constant fear; the dread of it was a thorn in their flesh, summer and winter. What if the seed did not grow, if the fruit did not ripen; what if their few cattle perished or the salmon did not run or the herring not come inshore? Yes, those were years that tried their souls as one bad harvest meant their utter destruction. They succeeded, prospered and multiplied because they placed all their confidence in the goodness and mercy of a kind and fatherly God, every moment of their lives, day and night.

The first year Alexander and his good wife, Catherine John Hugh, and their two sons lived in Cape Breton they lived on land belonging to a friend at the "front." They lived in a hut, hastily constructed of logs with a bark roof, a stone fireplace, no windows, their door a boat sail, their beds made of ground spruce and hemlock boughs and their chairs the two wooden trunks bought at Dunvaghan and containing all their earthly possessions. They suffered severely that winter, and here was born their third son, their first in the new world. The child was never well. That is why they bestowed upon him all the affection of their lonesome souls. He was gentle and handsome, but he withered away as the snows of spring and when nature was bespeckling the sunny spots with wild flowers and the swallows were nestling in the chimneys, he died. They buried him in sorrow after selecting the finest spot they and their neighbors could find, on the side of a little hillock facing the open ocean. Here within the hearing of the waves' gentle lullaby as it broke upon the clean sand of the shore below and within sight of the Cameron River as it calmly intermingled with the waters of beautiful Bras d'Or he was laid to rest. The hill itself was a spot of beauty, a garden of wild flowers, white and blue violets, golden eyed dazys, blue and yellow wild ireses, mint white clover, golden-rods and in back the virgin forest, grey spruce and white birch, all lifting their heads and arms to the sun and their

God, and those simple good people saw more of God's glory in those simple wild flowers than we do in the rarest cultivated plants, because vanity had not tarnished their beautiful lives. This spot seemed prepared in advance by nature to welcome the body of an angel and there they buried him as there was no ground consecrated by bishop or priest in the region. But they consecrated it themselves with their faith and simple obedience to God, by their affections for their son, by the sympathy and loyalty of their neighbors and by the water of their eyes. On the feast of Sts. Peter and Paul the first child of the district, the seed of the Barra-man mingled its ashes and dust with the red clay of Beaver's Cove. Big Alexander chiseled a grey granite field stone into which he crudely carved a cross and "W. N." the name of his child and placed it at his head.

* * *

Twilight was settling fast as Big Alexander left his friend, Hugh Hector's house that evening at Red Head. He walked east, about two miles, on land before he undertook to cross the ice to Beaver's Cove. It was a calm evening about the middle of winter, with light chips of snow in the air. Shortly after taking to the ice the snowfall thickened and as the night closed its curtains of real darkness over the earth, the snow was falling as thick as weeds in the widow's garden. Before he walked a quarter of a mile he could not see three yards ahead of him with the fast falling snow and the darkness of the night, and awhile afterwards, as I have already stated, he realized that he was absolutely and completely lost. He laid the bag of wheat in the snow and sat on it. He was wet with sweat and melting snow but while his body welcomed the rest his mind was busy reasoning the situation he was in. The Scot reasons slowly but generally correctly. He reasoned that he was nearer the Big Island than the Boisdale side but which side of him was either side he could not reason, nor which the Narrow's Stream or the Barrachois Gut. Therefore, he decided to wait the morning's light. Hours went by, long, lonesome hours. The night was growing much colder, his clothes were long ago frozen as steel armor. What a silent night, what a quiet country, was nature all dead or was it only fast asleep? He would welcome the call of the gull or the braying of a deer or the bark of a hound. He felt very tired and sleepy. He wanted to lay down in the snow and sleep. He was never so sleepy before. Big Alexander was hardy and wise in the things he knew but he did not know his Cape Breton; he did not know that he was slowly freezing to death.

It was in this stupor of cold and sleep he first saw "the light" —for a light with its brightness was breaking the terrible darkness and solitude of the night about him. A light with its vividness was awakening all his senses to the dangers of his perilous situation—a beautiful light, the emblem of hope, the emblem of God Himself.

Yes, someone had lit a fire on the shore to guide him. That was an old custom in the Hebrides when someone was lost at sea. Yet he doubted if he could see a fire from shore in this snow and blackness. It must be someone coming to meet him. He was sure of that now as the light was moving sharply from in front of him to his left. He must not lose that light. If he was facing the Boisdale shore according to the light he was very near the Narrow's Stream. If the light was facing the Boularderie side he was not far from the Gut. He got to his feet with a painful effort, fighting off the dreadful stupor and chill that enveloped his senses. He was stiff and numb, as if tied with a dozen chains. He swung his arms and stamped his feet, slowly walking around, swinging and dancing. Finally he felt that he could continue his journey so he shouldered his bag of wheat and faced the light.

Where was it leading him to? The Big Island or the Boisdale shore? It did not matter. Light meant warmth, human beings, safety. He knew at least it wasn't into the open sea.

He walked and walked and walked. Slowly at first but as the warm stream of blood started coursing through his body bringing strength to his legs he gradually gained speed and stride. The light was always in view, never very far away, never within speaking distance, much larger than a star but not as large as the moon. He wondered why he was not catching up with it after traveling such a long distance. The snow storm was now clearing but the night was much colder. He did not mind the frost anymore as he was warm walking in the deep snow. He must have traveled two good miles when suddenly he noticed he was gaining on the light. Yes, he was sure of it. The light was nearer him now than ever before only when he saw it first out there on the ice. He speeded up to know his benefactor but the next moment the light disappeared. As it did, he saw that he was on land. He could make out the forms of trees with their cover of snow, and he was entering an open space up from shore. He thanked his God that he was safe on land. "After all," he said to himself, "the light must have been from a window to guide me and the house must be near at hand, according to where I last saw the light." So he climbed the hill and scanned the open field everywhere for a cottage or a broken pathway among the trees surrounding the opening. While climbing up the hill he stopped abruptly as he saw an object in the snow he well remembered. He knelt down to examine it more closely. It was indeed "the stone," a grey fieldstone, into which was crudely carved a cross and the letters "W. N."— his son's grave.

Chapter 2

The Long Road

P. McE. Nicholson

F or many, many miles around, the Loon Lake region was known not only for its wild beauty but also for its quaint people. There were many other lakes in the district; Loch Allen, Gillis Lake, MacAdam's Lake, Loch Donald Allister, but Loon Lake was "The Lake" generally understood when people spoke of mysterious happenings, ghosts and fore-runners. So also was the "Big Glen" spoken of with a marked degree of respect and awe in comparison with other glens in the district. There were the North Glen, the Owl Glen, Glen Avarrish, but the "Big Glen" was "The Glen" from which centered important reckonings. Was this because its valley was a little more fruitful, its trees taller and stouter, its wild berries more luxurious and sooner ripened, its grass a little bluer, its potatoes a little mealier; or was it because its early settlers, Islanders from the Hebrides, were more learned in the signs that come only from raw nature, the deep merciless sea, the virgin forest, the unbroken soil, the seasons coming and going with their bitter and sweet, and finally their sole dependence on the mercy and goodness of a fatherly God whose guidance and assistance their lives depended every minute of the

197

day and night? Quaint people I say, rather mystic. They see and read causes and readily learned what God directed their course through those slight tokens of understanding that we of later generations call superstition.

There was a time in the life of the Loon Lake region when priests were few and far between, and when there were no doctors at all. Peculiar stories could be told of those days. Skeptics would laugh at them; learned men would doubt them; but common folks who live very close to nature accept them without question. There was the time when big Norman said his confession to a huge stone and at its conclusion the great stone crumbled into small fragments. There was the Good Friday John Newel in defiance of the moral custom of the village went into the woods for ash-staves and found to his dismay blood oozing from the first sapling he put his ax to. There was the night Mary Sandy died leaving behind a two week old child. The family's only cow though barren for four months had plenty of milk the very next morning. Yes, peculiar stories among quaint people but people simple and honest, trusting in a superior, loving power with all the trust and confidence of absolute and unquestioning faith.

Michael Laughlin, the Barra-man, was a pioneer when the Loon Lake district was still young. In fact, he with his good wife Catherine and their first three children were the first to settle in "The Glen." He was a hardy Islander from the Outer Hebrides, and he loved the sea as the gulls love the billows. So cutting down the huge trees, clearing and burning patches of the virgin forest into potato and oat fields were labor not to his liking. But love lightens labor and with Catherine constantly at his side, gradually, open spaces appeared among the trees. A comfortable log-hewed home was erected with a shed for his cow and hens and a "greeness" for his vegetables. As the years went by, the patches of green among the trees became a fruitful, fertile farm.

The log home became larger and taller as the family also became larger and stronger. Their wants while not numerous were bountifully supplied. They were rich because they were contented, happy because envy had not marred their simple life. Their lot was the lot of all "The Glen." When sorrow entered into any family, "The Glen" shared that sorrow alike. Joy was the same. You might say they were uncouth, without culture, but theirs was a culture of a high but forgotten degree. Is it culture to keep the Ten Commandments, to love your neighbor as yourself, to suffer little children to come unto Him in their natural course of time, rather than selected according to convenience? Yes, in the Loon Lake district culture was measured in very large bushels, large families, kind hearts and hearty smiles.

I said Michael Laughlin liked the sea and he found time each year to spend some months at the occupation of his youth —deep sea fishing. Shortly after his coming to "The Glen" when his planting was finished and his fences repaired, he would journey to the Bar and engage himself out on some sailing vessel during the summer months, when fishing for him was a joy and profit. Later, on a well equipped vessel, the "Mary Ellen," he made several very successful trips to the Grand Banks off Newfoundland, the best cod-fishing spot in the whole Atlantic Ocean. This meant to him and his family a little money and more food in winter.

One year in particular, in fact, the eighth year after his coming to "The Glen" and the year of the "Great Event," he received word that the "Mary Ellen" was sailing for the Grand Banks the following Thursday at six o'clock in the morning, and that he was expected with pleasure to join the crew by then. With mighty good will he applied himself with the finishing of his late planting as it was a late spring. Finally, the Wednesday evening preceding, contented that his work was well done, he bid God's blessing to his Catherine and his five children and started his twenty-odd long Scottish miles on his journey to the Bar and the "Mary Ellen." This journey he must travel in seven hours and being a strong man in the prime of life, traveling in the cool of a June bright night was preferable to the warm sunlight. He left with a light heart and a firm step, confident that God would guard his family and himself until they would meet again.

If coming events cast their shadows beforehand, the Barra-man that night was not aware of it. It was a peaceful calm night in late June. As he turned the north-east side of majestic Loon's Lake, that inland sea, a mile and a half high above sea level, its bosom as smooth as a maiden's cheek was gleaming beautifully in the mellow light of a full moon that made the night almost as bright as day. In the midst of the picturesque lake is an island covered with balsams and seldom visited by a human being. Here the wild loon makes its nest every year, and being a night as well as a day bird, the only ripple on the water was a flock of these shy birds feeding on lake trout. The only noise to break the silence of the night was a shrill call of the mating bird high over the water answering from the deep shadows of the bushy island. Michael Laughlin smiled to himself. He knew nature and loved it, because over it all he saw the infinite plan of the Creator at work, unfolding itself as a weaver weaves a pattern— sometimes mysterious, sometimes understandable but always bringing out the perfect design.

By two o'clock in the morning, Michael Laughlin arrived at the forks where a blazed trail left the main road near the foothills of Mt. Morrison. The main road dipped south by east along the valleys of the McCleod River while the blazed trail continued in a straight easterly line up and down hill, over streams, deep gullies, girding the ridges of Glen Avarrish and across the steep Morrison. It was a hard road to travel but shorter by six miles when again it joined the main road at

Ridges Creek. He took the trail without hesitancy as every moment of time and every unnecessary step were precious for the completion of his journey. On top of Bain Ardth, one of the highest peaks of the Morrison, and before dipping into Glen Na-Shea, he paused to look over this new majestic land so much like his own beloved Scotland; mountains and valleys, lakes and streams, all so new, so untouched by man. Trees and trees were in every direction. There was the deep green of the spruce and hemlock, the paler green of the young birch, beech and maple. Here and there a cluster of white flowers of the dogwood and the wild cherry could be seen. A slight fog followed the McCleod seaward marking its course like a white ribbon running in a mass of dark green. The moon was now dipping sharply westward, its light slightly waning as in the east the deep blue sky was taking on a tint of rose. Not a murmur of noise nor a rattle of wind could be heard. It was the hour before dawn, the hour all nature is asleep. Michael Laughlin marveled at what he saw and humbly removing his bonnet he reverently blessed himself, knowing that he was in full sight of the marvelous work of God.

Traveling on the eastern side of Bain Ardth was much easier as it sloped in his direction and the forest was not so thick though the light of the moon was less clear. His path was now in deeper shadows. The Barra-man walked briskly as does a man sure of himself and at peace with the world. What his thoughts were we can only surmise. Were they of his family, since every step he took lengthened the distance between them; or was he speculating on the success of the summer work; or was his mind far away in the country where so many of his friends still lived and where his parents were buried? He was, however, humming a Gaelic boat song which was abruptly stopped as a hand was placed on his shoulder and a voice spoke clearly and distinctly near him, saying, "Michael, return to the forks and take the long road." Through his mind shot the absurdity of such an act. He had already traveled two-thirds of the distance of the trail road. He was on the downgrade side of the mountain. Furthermore, to return to the forks and take the main road now to the Bar would jeopardize his chances of arriving on time to join the crew of the "Mary Ellen."He answered quickly, "Indeed I will not," at the same time drawing aside as if from the gentle touch on his shoulder. The next moment he realized that he was absolutely alone. To his knowledge, no human was within two miles of him. He looked keenly in every direction, seeing no one and hearing nothing except distant notes from the whippoorwill as the dawn was now breaking. Without further ado, he continued calmly on his journey. He traveled about a quarter of a mile further, perhaps with added speed, as the thought of this imaginary request and the folly of it vexed his mind, when again that same gentle touch and that same voice, perhaps a little stronger, commanded him, "Michael, return at once to the Forks and take the long road." Again Michael answered, "No!" His answer was firm as of one who had made a decision and meant to keep it. In his mind, he thought someone was following him and was trying to fool him. There was a patch of clear opening across the road a little ahead. On the other side, there was a group of willows. He thought to himself, "I will cross the open space, hide in the willows, and watch the road. Whoever is following me must cross that space and I will see him." This he put into execution at once.

For the lapse of ten minutes, he waited silently under the cover of the mountain willows, his eyes glued to the road, but no intruder appeared, no noise broke the silence of the calm summer morning. The birds were now all singing their morning matins in unison—the whippoorwill, the oriole, the robin, the chattery bluebird, the coy wood sparrow, and further down the hill the ceaseless harmony of the bog orchestra—the frogs. At last Michael Laughlin was satisfied that he had eluded the intruder that was playing pranks on him, and again he took to the trail. This time he walked more cautiously, with measured steps, with eyes and ears alert to detect any foreign disturbances. He had scarcely traveled two hundred yards when again he was forcibly halted. A firm grip was on his shoulder. He was spun half around like a top and faced the hill he had just descended. He was again asked by the same firm voice, "Michael Laughlin are you going to return and take the long road?" "No I'm not," he answered. He was physically detained and distinctly spoken to, and yet he could not see, in the early morning light, anything of human character. Only trees in every direction, an open trail, a stone here, a boulder there, dead leaves mingling with green moss and young shrubs in their tender leaves. The next moment he was lifted off the ground— yes, lifted some twelve feet, then thrown down with great violence. He landed on the trail, limp and useless, every bone in his body as if broken, every muscle aching, his senses, however, all keen and active, seeing, hearing, thinking, but he had not enough strength to rise. The voice spoke again. There seemed more of complaint in it this time. "Michael, will you return now?" The Scot is generally more logical than sentimental. The Barra-man knew he was licked and took it. "Yes," he answered, "I will now return"—and he did.

Michael Laughlin lived in "The Glen" a long useful life, respected and loved by all, young and old. He came to be considered as a patriarch in his later years and he looked the part in his long flowing beard and white hair; but the smile of happiness was still young in his keen eyes, and his hand was as eager as ever to help a neighbor. He died at the ripe old age of ninety-four, surrounded by twelve children, seventy-two grandchildren, and nearly two hundred great-grandchildren—all useful citizens of the Loon Lake district. Fishing he carried on as usual for many a year, during the summer months—fishing, but shore fishing.

Oh yes! The "Mary Ellen" sailed that memorable June morning without Michael Laughlin. Three weeks later while on her return trip, she was caught in a severe storm off the south coast of Cape Breton, and was broken to pieces on the rocks of Scatteree. The "Mary Ellen" with her crew of seventeen perished and found untimely graves at the bottom of the sea.

But, Michael Laughlin, the Barra-man had obeyed and had taken the long road.

Chapter 3

The Brothers

P. McE. Nicholson

etween the years of 1870 and 1890 the Loon Lake
Country, particularly the "Big Glen," reached the
zenith of its greatness. By then the third generation in
the Glen (descendants of the hardy Scottish Catholic Islanders
from the Outer Hebrides) were opening new farms, building
new homes. The blazed trail and the bridal paths had long given
way to good wagon roads joining village to village, to church, to
store, to school, to harbor. The saddle was replaced by wagons
and carts. The "Chas Chrom" and the hoe were replaced by
steel plows. The adze, the "Bal Sobhaidn" also the hand-
propelled grist-stones were replaced by water power mills which
could be found on almost every stream. The cheerful open
chimney was boarded up and in its place were cast-iron black
stoves (generally the Waterloo of the Niagara). Kerosene lamps
took the place of the "cruisgein" or the tallow candles, and the
"aithinne" by lanterns. The hand loom was on its way out and
store clothes were becoming fashionable. The "Glen" was prosperous and did not know it. The family that did not harvest
between eighty and one hundred barrels of potatoes was rare—
other vegetables accordingly. In the Fall a steer or two were

slaughtered and corned down for the winter. A pokey was slaughtered before Christmas and another before Easter. Tripe and puddings (black and white) were prepared and partly cooked and hung in rows on wooden pegs in the attic, and to climb to that attic would do you good by the smell of mint, wild sage, and caraway seed.

Besides eating "high of the hog" in those years it was also about as happy a spot as you could find on earth. Between the end of Advent (at Christmas) and the beginning of Lent (Shrove Tuesday) it was a continual rounds of match-making weddings, tucking frolics all throughout. There was hardly a house that did not possess a fiddle and often a set of bagpipes. Music and dancing reached a high degree. To see a "Single Four" danced by two men and two women to the music of "Christie Campbell" or "Cober Faidn" would lift your thoughts and emotions into seventh heaven, and the better songs of the different clans were sung with a feeling of loyalty and devotion.

However, that did not last. If progress is the life blood of nations it was the death knell of the "Big Glen." Stories of successful men from the neighborhood who were making good away were seeping in—men such as MacAskil of St. Ann's, Jack Munroe in Montana, Klondike Dan in the Yukon, Neil MacNeil in Boston, the MacLeans, sea captain brothers sailing the Pacific Coast (was the Sea Wolf), and many others. Fame and fortune were beyond the hills and valleys of the "Big Glen." The young became discontented, the old discouraged. By 1910 the "Big Glen" was like the "Deserted Village" of Milton and nature and the forest set in to claim its own. Still while there is living a descendant of that "Happy Glen," the "Big Glen" will live to share its culture, its hospitality, its love for everything Scottish wherever they are, and stories of its simple honest life, its wit, its fidelity to one another, and yes, its supernatural side come to mind from time to time.

Big Donald's farm was one of the finest farms in the community. It was now owned by the third generation, Young Donald and his brother Alex (Big Donald's grandsons), but it was still called the "Big Donald Farm." It was very productive, sloping south by southeast toward the river, facing the early sun and sheltered from the north winds by the Boisdale Mountains. By hard work and prudent management, their houses and stock and farm implements were the best in the district. Young Donald was married and had a small family, but Alex was a bachelor, living in the old home as one of the family and you could never know who held ownership of the farm as they worked together step by step, consulting and agreeing always.

One summer after planting, as was his custom, Alex went to the mines to work for a month or two. He was strong, healthy, and sturdy and the money he earned was always also applied to the house and farm. They were a peaceful, helpful, good people respected by the community. In early August that year, Donald Ban had occasion to go to town with a horse and carriage and while a distance of about a mile and a half from his home he met Alex on his way walking home. They stopped and chatted for awhile and Donald Ban wanted to turn around and both of them drive home but Alex would not listen to him, saying, "You go about your business—I'll walk home and take my time."

So they parted, but as Donald Ban was leaving, Alex asked him, "How is the grain field, and is the sty still up?"

Donald Ban answered that the grain was starting to ripen and that the sty was still up and that the neighbors were walking around the field.

Alex said, "Donald, take down the sty as soon as you can. There will be many grain fields and paths through them after we are all dead and gone."

"Well," said Donald, "we can talk that over when we will get home."

A Man in Overalls

As Donald Ban went his way with as much speed as possible so as to get back home, he could not take his mind off his brother. Alex looked pale and haggard. Why didn't he let him know he was coming home as usual so he could meet him at the station? Why, come to think of it, had he no grip for his extra clothes, no parcels as usual for the children and, above all, why so emphatic about the sty on the path through the grain field? Yes, Alex himself had suggested and built that sty. In those days, and perhaps still today, there were footpaths from house to house—short-cuts as it were, and perhaps you could walk for miles without going near the main roads. But if sometimes a grain or potato field was planted where this path was going through, a sty was put up at the edge of that field indicating that until that sty was taken down travelers had to go around the field to save it from being tramped upon. When the brothers prepared this certain field and planted it with wheat in the spring, Alex insisted on putting up a sty and now he was all for removing it. It all seemed strange.

Donald Ban arrived back home in the early afternoon. On driving down through his farm from the road to his home, he noted with pride the results of their labors in large grain fields, now taking on the deep yellow of ripening grain, potato fields in healthy stock covered with white blossoms—reminders of new potatoes already forming at their roots—the deep green of turnip and carrot tops and the lighter green of cabbage. There were so many reasons to be grateful to a kind and bountiful God—so much beauty in the "Big Glen." Nature was so kind to it—fertile soil, well watered by crystal springs—healthy and contented neighbors—a school and a church six miles away, yet, you could hear its bell chiming the "Angelus" and the hour before Mass on Sunday mornings, the tone reaching from hill to hill, from mountain to mountain in a continuous symphony of music growing deeper and fainter as it rolled off into space unknown through light pure air.

From his deep daydreaming, he noticed that his horse had stopped at the hitching bar and that his wife and children were coming out of the house to meet him. He knew at once that there was something wrong by their sorrowful tear-stained faces, and his wife was holding in her hand a yellow slip of paper—"A Telegram" which she was waving back and forth as something hateful yet something real.

"Annie," he said, "what in the Name of God is wrong?"

"Donald," she answered, "Alex is with us no more—he was killed in the mine this morning."

She could not say anymore with the grief that filled her bosom as she handed him the yellow slip of paper addressed to him from Sydney Mines.

"Woman," Donald answered, "that is not so—that cannot be as I have spoken . . ." but the sentence he never finished as his eyes glanced hurriedly over the printed words: "TO DONALD BAN MACDONALD — REGRET TO INFORM YOU THAT YOUR BROTHER ALEX MET WITH A MORTAL ACCIDENT IN THE MINE THIS MORNING AND ABOUT AN HOUR AFTERWARDS (9:30 AM) PASSED AWAY. PLEASE ADVISE ETC. ETC. SIGNED THE MINE MANAGER."

"My God! This cannot be. There must be a mistake," Donald said, as in his own mind he was saying again and again, "wasn't I talking to him in the flesh on the road about a mile away, and about the time he was supposed to have had that accident? What is wrong? Wouldn't I know my own brother? It was so real—yet, the yellow paper in his hand was also real. Its communication was not a joke, but information and a question asking for instructions as to internment."

At last he said to his wife, "I must leave for the Mines at once to make arrangements to bring my brother home."

But instead of unharnessing the horse or of taking a bite to eat, he went to an out-house, took down a scythe and walked calmly to the grain field, and after taking apart, pole by pole the sty, and piling it orderly across the newly formed path around the field, he mowed a furrow along the old path through the ripening grain. Then he paused at its end and said as if for the world to hear, "Alex, dear brother, how true, how true; there will be many a grain field with paths through them for the convenience of its neighbors after we are all dead and gone. So, dear Soul, Rest in Peace."

Chapter 4

The Heavy Load

P. McE. Nicholson

The Loon Lake country, particularly the "Big Glen," was widely known for many and various reasons. It was, first and foremost, as Scottish as the Stone of Schone or the Sword of Wallace. It was as old as the songs of Ossian, the tales of Fionn MacCumhail, the peobrach of MacCrimmon, the faith of St. Calamn Gillie. It was as young as the virgin forest, the unbroken soil, the undiluted spring rumbling freely over creg and dell down the mountainside. In the morning it was full of hope, of strength, of courage and of faith; in the evening it was lonesome after friends and relations thousands of miles beyond a friendless sea. Lonesome for their native glens and lochs, mountains and streams; lonesome for their hounds and guns, their boats and nets, their cattle and sheep, their crofts and cottages, and above all their sheilings on the mountainside. Yet, over it all, was a deep and passionate love for God—a childlike faith in his protection and a sincere good fellowship with all human beings—which mocks and scorns our materialistic and atomic age.

Among the forty-odd families that settled here about 1837, there were as many representative clans and sects as ever met at the Mods at Sterling or the Games at Inverness. Clans that feuded and held enmity for thousands of years lived here side by side—good friends, good neighbors—Campbells of Argyle, MacDonalds of Glencoe, Camerons of Lochaber, MacLeans of Lochbuiah, Barrach, Uistiest, Morariar—all clan difference and rivalry was forgotten because to them the clanship was dead—in fact, it died twice—once on the bloody field of Culloden, with their loyal and beloved Chiefs, and secondly, as they sailed down the Mul of Kantire to the open sea. But a new clanship was taking root—a clanship stronger than blood or name, a clanship formed in the fire of adversity, in the contest to survive, in the constant struggle with stubborn nature, the fear of hunger, of sickness, as they cleared the forest, built homes, raised families—a clanship as firm today as the bosoms of every descendent of those people wherever they live—a clanship you could not understand if you were not born in the Loon Lake country.

There were people in the Loon Lake Country like John and Collin, the Bards, and the Red Curries who could compose Gaelic poetry of excellent merit at the drop of a hat and claimed their ancestors received this gift hundreds of years before them from "Na Schaniech" or "Fairies;" and there were the Morrisons who could play the pipes with good quality at that, when they were old enough to lift a chanter and blow into it. They also claimed this gift of music was given their ancestry by a Fairy Prince in a rocky cave in Inverlochy. There was a certain family of whom the oldest male heir could cure any stage of cancer if it was external, where he could treat it with plasters of his own making, receipt for which was in the family for hundreds of years. There were people who could cure a toothache, a sty, a sprain—people who could see coming events like weddings and funerals beforehand and called it "second sight." There were people who could take the butter out of your churn and others who could counter-check them—all through reciting some rhymes or prayers, forgotten today as far as I know. All that was also as Scottish as the Stone of Schone or the Sword of Wallace.

Johnny Angus left his home at Castle Bay that morning at the break of dawn. It was after the thaws of Saint Patrick in the latter part of the month of March and most of the snow was gone. That which remained was well frozen in the early morning and walking was indeed very good. He was dressed in home-woven gray woolen homespun, on his head a Balmoral Bonnet, and his feet well covered in a pair of well-worn shanks, made from the hide of the hind legs of an ox or cow and laced with eel's skin. He had neither dog nor gun but there was an urgency and haste in his every step and the look of anxiety on his face as he headed for the "Big Glen" in the Loon Lake Country some seven or eight miles away. He passed Eskasoni Village where a large number of Micmac Indians were camped for the winter, taking advantage of the good hunting in the dense forest surrounding them and the good fishing always of some kind to be found in the beautiful Bras d'Or Lake. After a while, he followed a path along the Indian River, a beautiful stream cutting the "Big Glen" in half with its origin flowing from Loch Allain near the midst of the Loon Lake Country.

As the rays of the sun crowned as of gold the lofty top of Ben Aird, the highest peak of the Morrisons, he noticed smoke curling up from the chimney of a cottage above the road and there he decided to call. He entered with the familiar salutation, "God be here." It happened to be the home of Ian Due and he and his good wife, Sarah, were having their morning repast of oatmeal scones and tea.

"God be with you," they both answered in unison and Ian Due continued, "Come up to the fire young man, partake of a cup of tea, and tell us your news."

"I will gladly take of your tea," said Johnny Angus, "but eat or delay I must not as I am on an urgent mission, unless you may direct me toward that which I so earnestly quest."

"Sit down, sit down young man, and eat of our fare, for whatever is done in too much haste is only partly done." This conversation, of course, was carried on in good Gaelic and Gaelic has depth and breadth of meaning that can never be expressed in English.

In the meantime, Sarah brought him a cup of hot tea and a goodly number of oaten cakes. After a little while Ian Due asked, "What now is the urgent mission you are on, my friend?"

"I was told by truthful men," said Johnny Angus, "that there is an eye-stone in this village and I would like to borrow it for a little while." He had as much earnestness in his voice and demeanor as ever was expressed by knight or slave in seeking for the Holy Grail.

"Three days ago my good wife went to the barn to milk a cow newly freshened and before milking her she gave her some grain and straw from the thrashing floor. Somehow, something went into her eye. She tried to get it out, and we are all trying to get it out but the eye is only getting worse. Now, the eye and the side of the face are swollen and she is suffering the pains of Purgatory. We had skilled men from Piper's Cove and even from the Narrows look at her but the more they pry the eye the worse it is getting. I don't mind her losing the eye if only the pain would cease but she hasn't rested or slept now for going on three days."

"Poor woman, poor woman," said Sarah, "Ian Due what can we do to help her?"

Ian Due pondered a long time then said, "There was an eye-stone in the Glen but I know it was lost at the front. But young man, you do as I tell you and you may get relief. After you finish this hasty meal continue further east for about one and one-half miles. To the left of the trail, you will notice a snug log cabin with a chimney coming out from the roof near the back and a ladder alongside of the house. Enter that house and tell them the mission you are on and that Ian Due, the miller, told you to call and ask for their help.

Johnny Angus left Ian Due's house with a heavy heart. If the eye-stone was lost what could he do or what could be done to help his wife until he could get a doctor from somewheres? Doctors were not so numerous then as now. He might even have to bring his wife to Halifax and that was not an easy task for a poor man to do without much money. Traveling was also a big obstacle. It meant rowing in a boat around the Island of Cape Breton, around Guysboro to Halifax. The St. Peter's Canal was not yet open. Shortly after leaving and while pondering on his gloomy situation he heard a hail from behind him and looking back he saw Ian Due coming his way. When he came up with him he said, "I decided to go with you. I might be able to do something for you which you might not be able to do alone."

With that remark they walked on together silently, each thinking his own thoughts. Finally, they reached the house already described and they entered. "God be here," Ian Due said as they entered the cottage. It was a snug warm clean house, small but comfortable. There was a large open fireplace at the back of the house in which was a good fire of wood briskly burning. It would hold a good quarter cord of wood. Near the corner of the fireplace, an old lady in her late eighties was sitting on a wooden chest knitting socks. She was neatly dressed in black, her snow-white hair parted in the middle, nicely combed, and covered with a black bonnet. Around its edges was a frill of white linen, starched and ironed, and over her shoulders was a snug woolen shawl.

There were two younger women in the house, likely her daughters, busy about their housework. The men folks were not visible.

"God be with you," they answered and the younger woman said, "Ian Due, we did not expect a visit from you today but Mother told us yesterday evening that early this morning a stranger would come to the house from the west, carrying a heavy load. This must be the man we were watching for but I do not see that he has a load of any kind on his shoulders."

"Molly, you are wrong and your mother was right," answered Ian Due. "Our loads may not be in pounds or bulk, nevertheless they can be heavier than either. This man is carrying a load that is heavy and hard to bear because he cannot rest from it a single moment until help comes his way and that is why he is here and that is why I came unexpectedly with him." Taking a chair he sat alongside the old lady. A short conversation took place between Ian Due and the old lady to which Johnny Angus did not pay any attention until he heard the old lady saying, "No! No!"

She said, "I promised Father Alexander MacSween that I would not do that anymore. I never broke my pledge and I will not now."

Ian Due spoke, "The Pharisee saw and went by, the priest saw and went his way, but the Samaritan saw and compassion moved his spirit. He helped, and whom did the Lord praise?"

"Ian Due," said the old lady, "I like you. You have been very good to me and mine. I helped your mother when you were coming into the world and you in turn said the departing prayers over my good husband as he was leaving this earth. You closed his eyes and made his coffin but you are asking me to break my word—something I never did before."

"If it is a sin to heal the sick, to help one's neighbor, to lift the burden of those sorely tried I will gladly take it upon myself. You do this for me and I promise you will not regret it," said Ian Due.

"Very well, very well," said the old lady, "and may God help both of us."

"Amen!" said Ian Due. "What do you wish me to do?"

"Go to the spring and fetch me a pail of clean water," answered the old lady, and while Ian Due went after the fresh water she graciously folded her knitting needles and calmly put them away. She then opened the old wooden chest that she was sitting on and took from its depth two stones—rather pebbles—about the size of a goose egg, of dark gray hue that likely came off the shore of South Uist.

She took a pebble in each hand and kneeling at the pail of fresh spring water she dipped both hands in it, at the same time reciting a form of prayer or rhyme while rubbing the stones together under the water. She went through this ritual once, then twice, without any sign of outside effect. Then she stood up, dried her hands on her apron and she said regretfully, "This matter seems beyond me today."

Ian Due, laying his hand fondly on her shoulder said, "Please Granny, just once more."

Reluctantly, she knelt again at the pail of water and performed the same ceremony—slower this time and with more emphasis on each detail. Finally, she dropped one of the stones, and opening her mouth she took something off the tip of her tongue and placed it in the palm of the hand of Johnny Angus saying, "Poor soul, no wonder she was indeed in pain."

Johnny Angus looked on what was in his hand—about a half an inch of barley cockle covered profusely with puss and blood. Astonishment replaced bewilderment on his countenance, then understanding. He thought of his wife he left in pain a good nine miles away. He thought of the skilled men from the Narrows and Piper's Cove and Castle Bay who tried so zealously to help her. He looked around him as Ian Due was helping this dear old lady, so meek, so frail, so harmless, to her

217

seat by the corner of the fireplace—both strangers to him. He could not say a word. There was something here beyond his understanding—beyond his reason—something as old as the Druids under the oak trees and yet in his hand he was holding the venomous barley cockle with its toll of blood and matter. He put on his bonnet and walked out of the house without saying a word and headed home. The heavy load he carried to the "Big Glen" had disappeared as the fog before the rising sun and there was a smile on his face and joy in his soul.

Chapter 5

Just Off the Trail

P. McE. Nicholson

I t was indeed Archie Gillis who first brought it to my attention. That was many years ago, in fact, the year after Donald John Laughlin's death. While it seemed a phenomenon to the few who saw it at the time or knew of its existence since, to me, who knew well all the circumstances, it was as plain as the mid-day sun. I could have told this story long before now, but there are things too secret, too awe-inspiring to talk flippant about. A heavy sigh, a lump in the throat, a burning tear are mediums of expression more eloquent than words. Have you ever met a priest carrying the Precious Host to a dying sinner? The God of Love and Mercy going in all humility to comfort and forgive his creature, while in a moment that same creature must stand before the Majestic Omnipotence of the Creator of all things to be judged. Conflicting emotions— sadness for losing a departing human being; gladness to know of a soul leaving in God's friendship; awe for the terrible judgment —but this is all ahead of my story.

The year 1900 broke most favorably in the Big Glen as well as all over the Loon Lake country. In early April, green blades of grass were growing stealthily in shady places, and near the springs the white violet was bravely showing its face to the sun from its green bed of moss. The bluebirds were quarreling as usual from bush to bush, while a few robins were already looking over prospects for their summer home. Gentle thaws after St. Patrick's Day melted the snow, and little brooks were discharging briskly the hillside waters into the Indian River that flows serenely westward down the Eskasoni Valley and into Castle Bay. An early spring was indeed in the offing and the quaint peasantry was taking advantage of it. On Palm Sunday, James John and the Blacksmith set the price to be charged on oat seed—their yearly custom—and planting was entered into with vigor. But Angus John, the Big Glen's weather prophet, often shook a gloomy head and said, "This weather cannot continue; all the signs are against it. There was a long spring after Easter; the rabbit has not shed his coat of white; the planet Mars is rather near the Twin Castor and Pollux in Gemini and the spring moon is entering far into summer. It cannot last—it will not last." But regardless, the fine weather continued unnaturally warm and fair until within one day of May Day, and then the fury of nature was unleashed with devastating effect upon an astonished and unprepared world.

That May Day was to be remembered ever afterward by the inhabitants of the Loon Lake country as, "the big day of the sheep," as hundreds of these useful domestic animals, newly shorn, together with their lambs perished in the unexpected and terrible storm. I have also occasion to remember it well, as I walked six long miles in the teeth of the easterly blizzard, wading nearly knee-deep in soft, slushy snow, to good old St. Andrew's Chapel to have our quota of seed blessed, as was then, and I hope still is, a beautiful custom among the devout Islanders and their descendants. Why, to be without blessed seed on May Day was like going without confession at Easter. The Catholic Scots of the Hebrides had many a noble custom, and chief among them was the dedication of their seed in the Spring time to the "God of the Planting," as well as in the Fall was the giving of thanks and homage to the "God of the Harvest." When man assumes to be master of his own destiny and accepts for himself full credit for his little achievements, then man is losing that affectionate bond that should exist between a kind Father and a wayward son; there is lost that understanding sympathy between a merciful Creator and His insignificant creature.

I journeyed back home with my neighbor, Donald John Laughlin, a little man in his late sixties. I would like to tell you much about this man for your own good. The world was hard on him, called him a failure, thriftless because he gave too much of his time and substance to others less fortunate, without pay or thanks; he had no bank account, no great herd of cattle in his stockyards, no modern home or barns, always poor, always yielding in a hard driven bargain, and always giving in to others point of view when no great principle was at stake. Yes, in yesteryears he was called a failure; he would be called a failure today, but to my mind he was the most successful man I have ever known. He was as healthy as an oak sapling. He was poor but never in want. I know that he loved his God passionately because he loved his fellow men dearly. There wasn't a sickness, a wake or a funeral but Donald would be there. If you were late in harvesting or short of seed at planting, Donald would give of his time and substance. If you needed a priest or doctor, or your wife a nurse, Donald was always ready day and night to help you. Yes, call him a failure if you will but I hope I will be some-wheres near him at the Banquet Table.

After climbing the Cove Mountains we paused at widow John James where Donald divided his blessed seed with the widow. At Neil, Donald divided again his seed in half, and at the crossroads, Rory Donald's wife was waiting to get a share of the fast-diminishing seed. Donald handed her the whole package after taking out a small part for himself, which he wrapped in his handkerchief. After she returned home, Donald and myself stood alone at the crossroads where we were parting. Donald was going east while I was going west and home. There was a deep silence between us. I thought I knew what was in his mind—the smallest share, empty hands, failure, disillusionment. Perhaps there was contempt in my voice as I said, "Donald, you have hardly any seed left. You better take some of mine." Donald looked up as if awakened from a dream. He looked at me and then beyond me and waving his hand over the land he said, "Patrick, this was a bad storm. There wasn't a half dozen people from this region in church today. Look at that beautiful wild country--down Loon Lake and beyond as far as the eye can see to the top of Ben Aird of the Morrison Mountains; then westward to Hugh Douglas and southward to Callin, the poet. All fine people in a fine wild country but all without blessed seed today." He drew his handkerchief from his pocket, unfolded it carefully, and in its center was one grain—a barley seed. He took a pace off the beaten path and kneeling in the snow he cleared a patch with his bare hands. He dug a hole in the earth and lovingly buried in it his last seed. He then covered it carefully and prayed a prayer I shall never forget! - "My Lord and My God, I have not much to offer you and much to ask. Bless the seed of Thy people, every grain that is planted and every grain that is to be planted and increase it a thousandfold and protect it to a ripe bountiful harvest. Mary, Mother of God, bless thy children and help them in all their needs, their bodies and souls. Joseph, who knows the cares and trials of a husbandman, keep watch and guard over them. Jesus, Mary, and Joseph, I am entrusting to your care the distribution of the merits of this blessed seed among all the people. Holy Trinity, bless our souls, keep our bodies and give everlasting glory to our departed friends." I was only a lad but I felt that this was more than a prayer—rather a direct request from a humble, trusting soul to a kind and generous God, Who could not refuse, Who would not refuse. I thought of Abraham praying for his children, of Moses in the desert asking for food for the children of Israel; of Lot crying over Sodom and Gomorra—yes, an echo from Calvary and the Cross: "Father, forgive them . . ."

The springs pass quickly into autumns and youth into mature manhood and old age. The years go by as if on wings and once again I stand at the crossroads at Rory Donald's, this time with my good friend, Archie Gillis. The Big Glen was as big as ever. I could see far away Ben Aird as if a sentinel, standing guard over the Loon Lake country; and westward to Hugh Douglas's, and southward to Callin's, the poet, but what an altered glen. It was silent, homeless, manless, absolutely deserted. The folks of my childhood were dispersed all over the world, from Glencoe in California, to Flanders Fields "beneath the crosses, row upon row." But most of them and those I loved the best were in St. Andrew's graveyard where the soft breeze of lovely Bras d'Or waves the golden-eye daisies that grow on their graves—Donald Laughlin among them. Perhaps his grave is unknown, perhaps without a slab to mark his last resting place, but Archie is speaking. He was talking all the time while my mind was pondering over many things. Yes, a lump in the throat, a tear crawling shamelessly down the cheek were my silent tributes to indelible memories. "I have watched that tree now for the past five years," Archie was saying. "Every summer it is covered with those glorious flowers from early June until late October. What kind are they? How did it come here? Who planted it in such an obscure place I do not know. But I do know that it is not a wild tree or a wild flower. It's more a rose tree than a rose bush and look at those flowers—examine them. Look at their perfect design, smell their lovely fragrance, what glorious colors, golden dawn, scarlet sunset, azure blue of the deep heavens and snow white of pure hearts . . ." Yes, that is it—snow white of a pure heart—Donald Laughlin's, kneeling on that very spot within an inch, in the snow and with his own bare hands planting his last blessed seed for the welfare of his neighbors.

Chapter 6

The Blacksmith

P. McE. Nicholson

Winter set in quite early that year. After heavy frosts that came early in December a good deal of snow fell before Christmas. But between the feasts of the Circumcision and the Epiphany a snowstorm raged unabated, accompanied by a strong north-easterly wind that covered the Atlantic seaboard from southern New England to Labrador and inland for about one hundred miles; a fall of snow that blanketed sections with an average of ten feet, the heaviest snowfall within the memory of men then living or since and in many sections of the country, that winter was known ever afterwards as the year of the "Big Snows."

Off the most easterly point of this continent lies Cape Breton Island and that snowstorm struck that island with great intensity. Some piles of snow were as high as twenty-five feet. Roads were blocked; traffic, and in fact, all activity was at a complete standstill for many weeks. People traveled between neighbors and stores on snowshoes and it was late in March before transportation was renewed in normal fashion.

In the beautiful fertile valleys of the Margaree River, conditions were as elsewhere throughout the island. But here the hardy farmers, descendants of Scottish Catholic Highland and Island immigrants, who one generation before settled here and hewed a home and a living from the virgin forest rather than take an oath of allegiance to a foreign king or false religion, soon had paths made for themselves to the village store, the parish chapel, and the village school.

Next to the priest, there was no one in the village within a radius of forty miles who was so highly regarded or respected as the "Blacksmith." As warden of the church, as trustee of the school, as overseer of the poor, roads and lands, and whenever work was to be done for the welfare of his neighbor, in fact for everything, the "blacksmith" could be counted on. Many a plowshare, a hoe, an axe, many a horse or ox he shod with or without pay. Many an argument he settled, domestic, political, land boundary, school difficulty, etc., with cold reason or warm common sense. But if those failed he settled them firmly and definitely with his strong right hand. When the parish priest would be away or indisposed, the "Blacksmith" would say the rosary in Church during May and October, and to hear him say "The Stations" Friday afternoons during Lent was worth many a sermon on the Passion. The "Blacksmith" prayed with all his being, with his loud course emotional voice, the tears streaming down unashamed his rugged face. Oh yes, in those days men prayed in earnest and fervor, and finer still they sought first the " kingdom of God and His justice."

The "Blacksmith" had a family of three sons, of whom Neil was the oldest. Neil was a fine strong healthy young man at the age of fourteen. Since he was old enough to pick up a horseshoe nail he worked with his father in the forge. At the age of six he could work the billows back of the firebox, and as time went on, he developed into a first-class smitty. He could hammer a steel bar into a useful, beautiful article and at his present age he could weld a steel blade into an axe or adze and temper it to razor-like keenness. Neil had the good traits of both parents; the strong rugged honest qualities of his father, the pious gently qualities of his mother. His book schooling, however, received only secondary consideration. The "Blacksmith" would say, "Well, the youngsters (Donald and Alex) will receive all the education they can absorb. They can be professional gentlemen if they have the ability. But Neil, there's a lad for you. See the strength of his arms, see the determination and patience of his features, the keenness of his eyes, the judgment of his last blows." Many a piece of work is spoiled for the want of an extra blow or for a blow too many. "Why shouldn't he be a good blacksmith? His ancestors were blacksmiths in the Isle of Barra for two hundred years." So the "youngsters" went to school religiously; Neil only a week now and again when the planting was finished or until more important work required his service.

But the "Big Snow" of early January left the forge without much work that year, no horseshoeing, no sleigh-shoeing, no axes or canthook for lumber work. So Neil, for the want of anything better to do, went to school. His young brothers were already reading the classics—Homer and Virgil—while he was laboring through long division. Such is the way of God manifesting again and again His Will to those who have the wisdom to understand It and the happiness to abide by It.

Some seventy-five years ago, school books and the method of teaching were far different from that of today. First, each pupil was in a class by himself and could cover as much work as his ability would permit. Secondly, the school books contained much more work. Take for example the "Taylor Arithmetic." It began with digits and continued into high mathematics. But this particular arithmetic book had one error. When the printer was setting up the book, a problem which was supposed to be in Part XI was placed in Part IV. The error was not discovered in time but a note was pasted on the front flyleaf and a red line was drawn around the problem in question. Neil was about a month in school when one day the "Master" discovered him in deep meditation over his work. The teacher knew all his scholars. He knew those who were slated for higher scholastic careers, and gave them special attention. The rest were instructed in the three R's as much as possible. Neil, however, he knew would not be long in school, another two weeks at the most, and he wanted him to have the benefit of his time. So walking down to his desk he inquired about his difficulty. Neil pointed out this particular problem to him. The teacher explained quite kindly to him the fact of the error and told him to continue with the rest and leave this question alone until he would be seven more years in school. Later that same afternoon the teacher found Neil pondering over the same problem. That time he told him sharply not to waste his time thinking over a question he would never be able to make, and added, "I doubt if I can make that problem myself." Neil did not look at that page again that day but in the evening he took his slate and arithmetic book home with him.

The "youngsters" were fussing and quarreling about their homework that night as usual but Neil was quiet by himself, at his slate and arithmetic. They all retired in due time. Neil remained behind. Some time during the night the mother awoke and saw a light in the living room. She went in to see why the light was left burning, but Neil was working on his slate as they had left him. He promised to retire soon. No one knows what time he went to bed that night, if at all. In the morning the fire was lit and Neil was about the chores around the stable when the rest awoke. He went to school as usual that day with his younger brothers. After school opened, he modestly told the "master" that he could now solve that problem. The "master" invited him to the board and there with chalk worked out in detail the Grade XI problem to the astonishment of the teacher and all the pupils. When he finished, the teacher quietly and silently put on his cap, his big coat and his gloves and walked the mile to the forge where the "Blacksmith" was at work. "Blacksmith," he said, "you are a wise man, wiser than most of us in the common things of life but as ignorant as the rest of us in understanding the fathomless Will of God. You want the younger boys fitted for professional careers—perhaps a doctor and a lawyer—and you give them every opportunity to become that, but you say Neil must carry on the traditions of your family—a good blacksmith and a husbandman of the old home-stead. Well, you must change your plans. Do with the young-sters what you will but Neil must remain in school. I have taught school for thirty-five years, in the old country and in the new, but never have I seen a mind so clear in reasoning, so deter-mined to find out the truth and understand it, as Neil, and who are you to hide his genius beneath your bushel?"

* * *

Fifty-five years after the year of the "Big Snow" I was in a group of Catholic gentlemen from the Maritime Provinces attending a convention in western Canada. With me were a few clerics from Cape Breton Island, who, on their way back home, stayed off for a few hours in Toronto. We called at the Diocesan Chancery, made ourselves known, and asked to see His Excellency, the Archbishop. The chancellor was most kind to us and said the Archbishop would be pleased to see anyone from "Down East." "I will show you where he is," he said, "when he is home there are just two places where you can find him at this time of day—either in the Sanctuary of the Cathedral or . . . well, come this way."

He led us to the basement of the building which I took to be a garage. As we entered the room I knew immediately that we were in a typical Cape Breton forge. There was the familiar firebox with the bellows handle just along side, the anvil on a stout wooden block, the wooden tub (a barrel sawed in half) full of water for tempering or cooling purposes, hammers, tongues, and all the average equipment you might see in any roadside village smitty's place. But more striking was the man at the anvil. He was a grey-haired, tall, strong looking man. His eyes were keen but kind, his features showing patience and determination, and the way he was shaping an iron bar into hinges for an extra large door, undoubtedly the door of a church, proved to me that he knew when his job was thoroughly finished. There was an old shabby cap on his head, an old leather apron tied tightly around his waist, the sleeves of his shirt were folded up above his elbows, his arms were muscular, his face sweaty and grimy with coal soot, but his countenance was beautiful because he was happy—happy and at peace with himself and his God and his fellow men. As we walked further into the room, we saw who the man was. Here was that high ecclesiastical dignitary whose advice and council were sought by the leading statesmen of the Dominion of Canada, that brilliant scholar and mathematician, the undaunted shepherd of the largest English-speaking Catholic See in the British Empire, his Excellency the Right Reverend Doctor Neil MacNeil, Archbishop of Toronto.

"O the depth of the riches of the wisdom and the knowledge of God! How incomprehensible are His judgments, and how unsearchable are His ways!" - Romans XI, 33.

The Highland Immigrant

Cape Breton's Greatest Heritage
P. McE. Nicholson

I remember, I remember
From the days of long ago,
When the elders of our village
"Ceilidh" at our hearthen glow.
How my heart and mind would quicken
With the pleasure since denied.
You could almost smell the heather,
See the gathering of the Clans.

They told great tales of love and war,
Of stormy seas, of County fairs,
Of Fuinn and Ossian and the Bards
The Fiery cross, hill-men on guard,
Of swords, claymores, dirks of steel
Of druids at the oaken tree,
Of summer shielings in the glen,
Of granite castle, mountain dens.

Bleak the day they sailed away,
Those trusty, brave Highland men.

A Man in Overalls

Their homes and crofts in ashes gray,
Separated from their kith and kin.
Packed in filthy ships as slaves,
Torn from customs—native sod,
With no star or chart to guide them,
But their humble trust in God.

Flodden's Field or Culloden's blunder
Was not the cause of Scotland's plight.
But greedy chiefs—disloyal lords
That broke their covenant with the Gael.
They traded their clans for deer and sheep,
Accepted Saxons and their gifts,
Prolonged the day by Justice laws
When Scots shall rule their native sod.

The village elders all are gone,
Their souls interred in Tir-Nan-Og.
They dearly loved their native land,
Their bones denied its restful sod.
They left a heritage behind,
Of leaders in both brawn and brain
Would gladly die for Scotland's cause,
Then live and be as English slaves.

The lark is singing in their glens
The thrush upon the bramble tree.
But there are none to hear their song
No one to love, to care, or see.
The flowers on their heroes' graves
Are choked with grass and mossy weeds.
The laughter of children at play
Are gone beyond some foreign seas.

The Highland Immigrant

O Scotland, how can I forgive
What you did to my sires?
And yet, I quickly bare my head
As the bagpipe marches by.
I dress the pleated Highland kilt,
I sing the songs of Skye.
The land of Wallace and of Bruce
I love you - - with a sigh.

Cape Breton

The Hebrides of the West
P. McE. Nicholson

Cape Breton glens are broad and long,
Its heart a bubbling river,
Its hills are lofty, rocky strands
With pine and laurel summits.
Its Lakes are mirrors, "Arms of Gold"
The ocean salmon spawning,
The coy loon shelter in its folds,
The grey goose feeds at dawning.

Our folks were orphans from the Isles
From off the Barra Sea,
Disposed of crofts and cottages
They crossed the turbulent sea.
Built churches, schools and colleges,
Made laws to keep them free
And named their dearest land-marks
For the lonesome Hebrides.

They cleared the stubborn forest,
Burned the scrubby trees;

Cape Breton

Removed the rocky refuse,
Tilled the virgin fields.
Their tools hand-made and scanty,
They planted barley seed,
And Barley John renewed his birth
Beneath the Maple Leaf.

They came - the Donald's and the Collin's
The Ronald's and the Neils,
Kind neighbors close together
Where a hand-clasp binds the deal;
They left the "lord" his mutton,
The "chief" his scrawny deer,
The warden and the sheriff
And the death foretelling seer.

There are fires brightly shining
From the windows of our glens;
A welcome sign to our Kinsmen,
"The Breed of Noblemen"
From Mary's Well to John MacGroth
We call you o'er the sea,
For a Highland heart is warmest,
Where the Highland heart is free.

Loch Lomand sings the tucking songs,
Dunvaghan pipes MacCremmon;
Iona's faith as fresh and strong
As taught by Collam Gille;
Glencoe retells of Ossian's dog,
Boisdale of Loch Uist,
Our Gaelic is as pure as
The Gaelic of MacMhuirich.

Acknowledgments

Paddy Nicholson once said, "There was John in every single family that I know of. . . . But then they'd put nicknames on them." Paddy named his first son John, and he was called John Joe. Dan, Paddy's brother, named one of his sons John, and we called him Johnny Uncle Dan. Both John Nicholsons valued their family history and took the necessary steps to safeguard it. Their efforts made it possible for me to write this book.

My uncle, whom I called Father John, took me to Scotland and the Isle of Barra in 2003, planting in my heart the first seed of curiosity about my Nicholson clan and its history. In recent years, we talked on the phone for hours about his recollections of his father and their life in Baldwinville and Worcester. He gave me his father's letters, folklore stories, and many old family photographs. He advised and encouraged me every step of the way, and our friendship blossomed, together with our determination to see the work through to completion. I am amazed and proud of my grandfather's accomplishments and forever grateful to Father John for trusting me to tell the story of A Man in Overalls.

Johnny Uncle Dan lived in Sydney, Cape Breton, and taught sociology at Xavier Junior College (now Cape Breton University). He was deeply interested in the Gaelic culture of rural Cape Breton. In the 1960s, he taped interviews with my grandfather, his father, and several of their Nicholson cousins, all of whom grew up together on the land settled by their ancestors. Those tapes captured the rich oral history of Rear Beaver

Cove in the nineteenth and early twentieth centuries. Johnny Uncle Dan also interviewed my grandfather about his involvement in the Cape Breton labor movement before 1920. I'm immensely grateful to him, for without these recordings, such first-hand testimony would have been lost forever. Johnny Uncle Dan passed away in 2009, but his recordings are accessible through the digital archives of the Beaton Institute of Cape Breton University in Sydney.

I am indebted to some artistically talented friends who contributed their services to me. My second cousin, Wanda Nicholson, endorsed this project from the start. She drew the cover image of the young "Man in Overalls" and helped format the photo and illustration files. I appreciate her unlimited willingness to read the manuscript, always helpful and encouraging. I am also grateful to Suzana and Elaina White for drawing the maps and the Nicholson family descendant chart.

To the friends and family who so generously offered their time and insights at various stages of manuscript preparation, I owe special thanks. From the very first draft, Martha Schott voiced her resounding endorsement of the story, assuring me that my work would become a valuable family heirloom. She has read drafts with red pen in hand even while traveling and vacationing with her husband, John. As an experienced editor, Martha gave me clear and precise feedback on grammar and style. I am also grateful to my brother, Paul J. Kiritsy, who combed the Boston newspaper archives, helping to solve the mystery of the death of our great-grandmother, Margaret "Maggie" McEachern Nicholson. I appreciate the insightful comments of other readers, including my son T. J. and his wife Lizzy Roy.

I met my third cousin George MacLean when he offered to guide me to the remote site of our ancestral lands in Rear Beaver Cove. He and his brother Joe have mapped the farms that our ancestors deserted a century ago. It was a magical experience when we stepped onto the ground settled by Big Alex and Catherine Nicholson over one hundred eighty years ago. He later introduced me to his family and other Nicholson relatives living in Cape Breton. He has read the manuscript with the eye of a trained editor. George has a deep understanding of the subject, and for his time and enthusiastic encouragement, I am truly grateful.

During the years of the COVID-19 pandemic, much of the research for this book was undertaken from home using internet resources made available by the Beaton Institute at Cape Breton University. The staff of the Institute promptly responded to requests for record digitization, giving me ready access to their collections. Kathleen MacKenzie, archivist at the Angus L. MacDonald Library at St. F. X. University, provided me with correspondence between my grandfather and the Reverend Doctor Patrick J. Nicholson, which proved to be extremely important to my research. Likewise, Susan Cameron, Special Collections Librarian, provided me with a copy of Catherine MacMullin Nicholson's 1898 obituary.

Thanks to Catherine and Rannie Gillis, third cousins from North Sydney who shared their research and memories of the family of George Nicholson.

In August 2023, Calum and Rhoda MacNeil welcomed me into their Barra home. Calum has a wealth of information about the people and history of the Isle of Barra, and I am grateful to him for sharing his knowledge with me.

My mother Anne Marie (Ana Mae) Nicholson Kiritsy and her siblings Margaret and Jim shared their childhood memories and encouraged me to tell their beloved father's story. These "interviews" were heartwarming for all of us.

Finally, I thank my husband, Mark Roy, for encouraging me

to take the time and space required to pursue this challenge. Mark is a consummate reader of biography and historical nonfiction, and his comments and suggestions have made the final product better than it would otherwise have been. His endorsement means the world to me, and for that, I am humbly grateful.

Notes

1. A Boy and His Grandmother

1. P. McE. Nicholson to Monsignor Doctor Patrick J. Nicholson, undated, in the author's possession.
2. Ibid.
3. Patrick Nicholson, interview by John Nicholson, 1965, sound recording CA BI T-514, Beaton Institute Digital Archives, Cape Breton University, Sydney, NS, Canada. Other participants in the conversation included Roddie F. Nicholson, Dan Nicholson, and Hector MacLean.

2. The Isle of Barra

1. Branigan and Foster, *Barra and the Bishop's Isles,* 19.
2. Compton MacKenzie, "Catholic Barra," in *The Book of Barra,* 22.
3. Ibid., 9.
4. Tom Shields, "Island the Reformation Did Not Reach," *Glasgow Herald,* March 10, 1982, https://news.google.com/newspapers?id=8v89AAAAIBAJ&sjid=fkkMAAAAIBAJ&pg=4336%2C2068228 : (accessed August 23, 2021).
5. MacMillan, *To the Hill of Boisdale,* 547-567.
6. Moidart Local History Group, "The Glen Moidart Papers: List of Tenants of South Uist as per the Judicial Rental of 1798," http://www.moidart.org.uk/datasets/glenmoidart/19.htm : (accessed January 11, 2024).
7. Campbell, *The Book of Barra,* 233.
8. Black, *Culloden and the '45,* 192.
9. Campbell, *The Book of Barra,* 117-119; Branigan and Foster, *Barra and the Bishop's Isles,* 127-128.
10. Calum MacNeil, "Barra and its History: Through the Eyes and Ears of a Modern Seanachaidh," https://www.ssns.org.uk/wp-content/uploads/2019/10/04_MacNeil_Barra_2006_pp_66-90.pdf. Transcript of a presentation to the Scottish Society for Northern Studies in Barra, June 2006.
11. Campbell, Book of Barra, 126.
12. Campey, *After the Hector,* 367.
13. Ibid., 193.

3. Just a Question of Time

1. Branigan and Foster, *Barra and the Bishop's Isles*, 137.
2. Ibid., 139. Colonel Gordon of Cluny bought the Isle of Barra in 1840. He was a shrewd businessman from Aberdeenshire. With no personal attachment to the tenants or interest in their well-being, Colonel Gordon's goal was to buy the estate at a low price and turn a profit. Within a decade, his plan had failed. In 1850, he began to "clear" people off the land and ship them to Canada to make way for sheep farming. "Gordon paid their passage, but otherwise they were given nothing and had little left of their own to take with them. They arrived in Canada utterly destitute, and after receiving relief from the Canadian authorities were sent on westwards."
3. See chapter 1, note 3.

4. Big Alex Nicholson

1. Patrick Nicholson, "The Hill They Blessed." See Part II, page 193 of this book.
2. See chapter 1, note 3.

5. Finding Land of Their Own

1. Martell, *Immigration to and Emigration from Nova Scotia*, 10.
2. See chapter 1, note 3.
3. See chapter 4, note 1.
4. Dunn, *Highland Settler*, 114.
5. See chapter 1, note 3.

6. The Big Glen

1. Rev. A. A. Johnston, in MacMillan, *To the Hill of Boisdale*, xliv.
2. See chapter 4, note 1.
3. See chapter 1, note 3.
4. From an incomplete, unnamed folktale by P. McE. Nicholson, in the author's possession.
5. See chapter 1, note 3.
6. Hornsby, *Nineteenth-Century Cape Breton*, 52-54.
7. Ibid., 126.
8. Crown Land Information Management Centre, https://novascotia.ca/natr/land/grantmap.asp. The petition (#12350) and the Grant (#11065)

were obtained from the Land Services Branch, Nova Scotia Department of Lands & Forestry.

9. See note 6 above, 126.
10. See note 6 above, 128.
11. See chapter 1, note 3.

7. Legacy of the Barra Gaels

1. Canada, Nova Scotia, Antigonish Catholic Diocese, 1823-1905, *Family-Search,* https://www.familysearch.org/ark:/61903/1:1:JV33-9RJ, 1887.
2. MacMillan, *To the Hill of Boisdale, xxvi.*
3. See chapter 1, note 3.
4. Ibid.
5. Ibid.
6. Pam Newton, "Neil A. MacKinnon of Rear Beaver Cove," *Cape Breton's Magazine,* January 1, 1987.

8. Gaelic life and customs

1. Author Unknown, "Barra in 1620," in Campbell, ed. *The Book of Barra,* 38.
2. See chapter 1, note 3.
3. See chapter 7, note 6.
4. P. McE. Nicholson, to "My family and many, many friends, particularly the Nicholsons, have urged me to write down for posterity my knowledge of our ancestors, mainly the "Barra Branch" of the Nicholson clan, so that this lineage may be preserved . . . although I can modestly say that I know this subject better than anyone now living. Therefore I wish it now recorded and preserved for future generations," in the author's possession. The details provide the basis for the imagined ceilidh scene.

9. The Supernatural

1. See chapter 4, note 1.
2. See chapter 1, note 3.
3. Johnston, *Antigonish Diocese Priests,* 71.
4. See chapter 1, note 3.
5. Ibid.

10. Hardships

1. Dunn, *Highland Settler*, 116-7.
2. See chapter 1, note 3.
3. Caplan, *A Stone for Andrew Dunphy*, 15-28.
4. See chapter 1, note 1.
5. Patrick Nicholson, "The Long Road," see Part II, page 199 of this book.
6. MacMillan, To the Hill of Boisdale, 93-95.
7. Ibid.
8. MacKinnon, *Silent Observer*, 21. Christy MacKinnon was the daughter of John D. MacKinnon, "the local schoolmaster, in a one-room schoolhouse that served all the children of the Boisdale countryside." They lived on a farm near Boisdale. She was born in 1898. She wrote and illustrated stories about her childhood in rural Cape Breton.
9. Roddie F. Nicholson, interview by John Nicholson, 1965, sound recording CA BI T-22, Beaton Institute Digital Archives, Cape Breton University, Sydney, NS.
10. See chapter 1, note 3.
11. Ibid.
12. Catherine Gillis, grand-niece of Father Pat Nicholson, in conversation with the author, October 11, 2022.
13. See note 9 above.
14. See note 9 above; George MacLean, e-mail message to author, March 29, 2023.
15. See chapter 1, note 3.

11. A Labor Activist

1. Mellor, *The Company Store*, x-xiii.
2. Ibid., 1-2.
3. Ibid., 10.
4. Patrick Nicholson, interview by John Nicholson, 1965, sound recording CA BI T-34, Beaton Institute Digital Archives, Cape Breton University, Sydney, NS.
5. Ibid.
6. "Violence is Coming," *The Gazette* (Montreal, Quebec), July 7, 1909.
7. See note 1 above, 55-56. Father Jim Fraser was pastor of St. John's Catholic Church in New Aberdeen during the strike of 2009.
8. Ibid., 56.
9. See note 4 above.
10. Ibid.

11. Dutil and MacKenzie, *Embattled Nation*, 128.
12. "Executive Council," *Edmonton Journal*, September 18, 1917, page 11, column 2.
13. "Labor Congress Looking Ahead at New Problems," *Montreal Star*, September 22, 1917, page 5, column 1.
14. See note 4 above.
15. Ibid.
16. Ibid.
17. Ibid.
18. Ibid.
19. Cameron, *For The People*, 128; 146.
20. *Rev. Doctor Moses Cody, (address at the retirement of Msgr. P. J. Nicholson,* St. Francis Xavier University, Antigonish, Nova Scotia, March 28, 1954). Sound recording, Angus L. MacDonald Library digital collections, https://stfx.cairnrepo.org/islandora/object/stfx:18087?solr_nav (accessed April 29, 2024).

12. Sydney

1. Details of the dance where Paddy and Annie met, as well as Joseph MacPherson's reaction to Paddy, were related to me by my mother, her sisters, and her brothers.
2. Jack MacNeil, *From the Cove to the Glen*, 28.
3. Ibid.
4. Father John Nicholson, in conversation with the author.
5. Wanda Nicholson, granddaughter of Dan Nicholson, in conversation with the author.
6. "Passing of Beloved 'Doc Pat:' Great Loss to the University," *St. Francis Xavier University Contemporary and Alumni News*, 3 (4), December 15, 1965, 4.
7. Ibid., 5.

13. To the Boston States

1. Paul MacEwan, *Miners and Steel Workers*, 57.
2. Find A Grave Memorial, https://www.findagrave.com/memorial/182638868/thomas-brazell#view-photo=159725262 (accessed April 29, 2024).
3. http://www.saintmartinchurch.org (accessed April 29, 2024).
4. See chapter 12, note 4.
5. Ibid.

6. Maggie Nicholson was seventy-four years old at the time of her death in 1931, not sixty-four as reported in the *Boston Globe* or on her death certificate.

14. Worcester

1. "Rev. James T. Reilly," *The Boston Globe*, May 14, 1946, page 29, column 5.
2. "Official Blackout Procedure for New England States," *The Boston Globe*, January 5, 1942, page 12, column 1.
3. See chapter 1, note 1.
4. Shaw, "The Vanishing Folklore of Nova Scotia," *The Dalhousie Review*, 348.
5. Ibid., 343.
6. Monsignor Doctor Patrick J. Nicholson to P. McE. Nicholson, June 3, 1941, in the author's possession.
7. Ibid.
8. J. J. MacInnis to P. McE. Nicholson, November 11, 1941, in the author's possession.
9. See chapter 1, note 1.
10. See chapter 11, note 19, 304.
11. Patrick Nicholson to Msgr. Patrick J. Nicholson, 22 June 1952, RG 5/11/12522, PNP, STFXUA.

15. Leaving a Legacy

1. Xavier College was founded in 1951 as a satellite campus of St. F.X. Its growth over the years reflects its service to the growing population of industrial Cape Breton. Now known as Cape Breton University, the history of its development can be found at https://www.cbu.ca/about-cbu/history/ (accessed April 30, 2024).
2. See chapter 1, note 3; see chapter 11, note 4.
3. See chapter 11, note 4. The speaker refers to S. A. Saunders, *Economic History of the Maritime Provinces*.
4. Roddie F. Nicholson was the son of Hector and Bridget (Johnston) and lived most of his life in Beaver Cove next door to his sister, Katie Anne, and her husband Michael Baeg MacLean. Roddie was the blacksmith of the Boisdale district. Catherine Monica Nicholson was the daughter of George and Catherine (Johnston) Nicholson, and the sister of Monsignor Patrick J. Nicholson (Doc Pat). Refer to the Nicholson Family of Rear Beaver Cove diagram on pages xiv-xv.
5. Johnston, *Antigonish Diocese Priests and Bishops*, 97.

6. See chapter 12, note 6.
7. https://www.cbu.ca/community/beaton-institute/history-of-the-beaton-institute/ (accessed April 30, 2024).
8. Sister Margaret Beaton to P. McE. Nicholson, September 14, 1967, in the author's possession.

Epigraph Notes

Part 1: C. N. Parsons, *"Cuimhne"* | "Remembrance," 6-7.

Chapter 1: Rev. Patrick Nicholson to J. C. MacMillan, Jan. 2, 1946, RG 5/11/10797, PNP, STFXUA.

Chapter 2: Quoted in Compton MacKenzie, "Catholic Barra," in *The Book of Barra*, 11.

Chapter 3: P. McE. Nicholson, "The Highland Immigrant."

Chapter 4: See chapter 1, note 3.

Chapter 5: Jeremiah 29:5-5, New American Bible, Rev. Ed.

Chapter 6: P. McE. Nicholson, "The Hill They Blessed."

Chapter 7: Rev. Patrick Nicholson in Archibald J. MacKenzie, *History of Christmas Island Parish,* Introduction.

Chapter 8: See chapter 1, note 3.

Chapter 9: P. McE. Nicholson, "The Heavy Load."

Chapter 10: P. McE. Nicholson, "The Brothers."

Chapter 11: John Mellor, Company Store, xiii.

Chapter 12: Eugene V. Debs, Los Angeles Evening Post Record, Sept. 6, 1912, page 4, column 3.

Chapter 13: A Man in Overalls, Canadian Labor Leader, June 1, 1918.

Chapter 14: P. McE. Nicholson to John J. Nicholson, Sept 12, 1943, in the author's possession.

Chapter 15: P. McE. Nicholson to Rev. John J. Nicholson, July 10, 1963, in the author's possession.

Part 2: Shamus Y. MacDonald, "Land and Belonging," 29.

Bibliography

Black, Jeremy. *Culloden and the '45*. London: Grange Books, 1990.

Branigan, Keith and Patrick Foster. *Barra and the Bishop's Isles: Living on the Margin*. Stroud: Tempus Publishing, 2002.

Cameron, James D. *For the People: A History of St. Francis Xavier University*. Montreal & Kingston: McGill-Queen's University Press, 1996.

Caplan, Ronald. *A Stone for Andrew Dunphy: Narrative Obituary Verse and Song in Northern Cape Breton Island*. Wreck Cove: Breton Books, 2018.

Campbell, John Lorne, ed. *The Book of Barra*. Stornoway: Acair, 1998.

Campey, Lucille H. *After the Hector: The Scottish Pioneers of Nova Scotia and Cape Breton 1773-1852*. 2nd ed. Toronto: Natural Heritage Books, 2007.

Dunn, Charles W. *Highland Settler: A Portrait of the Scottish Gael in Nova Scotia*. Toronto: University of Toronto Press, 1953.

Dutil, Patrice, and David MacKenzie. *Embattled Nation: Canada's Wartime Election of 1917*. Toronto: Dundurn, 2017.

Hornsby, Stephen J. *Nineteenth-Century Cape Breton: A Historical Geography*. Montreal: McGill-Queen's University Press, 1992.

Johnston, Rev. A. A. *Antigonish Diocese Priests and Bishops: 1786-1925*. Edited by Kathleen M. MacKenzie. Antigonish: The Casket Printing & Publishing, 1994.

_____. "Boisdale Parish Historical Sketch." In *To the Hill of Boisdale*, by A. J. MacMillan, xliii-xlix.

MacDonald, Shamus Y. "Land and Belonging in Gaelic Nova Scotia." PhD diss., Memorial University of Newfoundland, 2017.

MacEwan, Paul. *Miners and Steelworkers: Labour in Cape Breton*. Toronto: Samuel Stevens Hakkert & Co., 1976. Accessed at http://www.archive.org.

MacKenzie, Archibald J. *History of Christmas Island Parish*. Antigonish: St. Francis Xavier University, 1926. Accessed at https://stfx.cairnrepo.org/islandora/object/stfx%3A11053.

MacKenzie, Compton. "Catholic Barra." In *The Book of Barra*, edited by J. L. Campbell, 1-25.

MacKinnon, Christy. *Silent Observer*. Washington: Kendall Green Pub., 1993.

MacMillan, A. J. *To the Hill of Boisdale: A Short History and A Genealogical Tracing of the Pioneer Families of Boisdale, Cape Breton, and the Surrounding Areas*. rev. ed. Sydney: Music Hill Pub., 2001.

Bibliography

MacNeil, Jack. *From the Cove to the Glen: A Conversation with Joe Neil MacNeil*. Big Pond: Breac Brook Press, 2019.

Martell, J. S. *Immigration to and Emigration from Nova Scotia: 1815 — 1838*. Halifax: The Public Archives of Nova Scotia, 1942.

Mellor, John. *The Company Store: J.B. McLachlan and the Cape Breton Coal Miners 1900-1925*. Canada: Breton Books, 2012.

Parsons, Catriona Nicìomhair. *Cridhe's Anam: Heart & Soul*. Halifax: Bradan Press, 2023.

Saunders, S. A. *Economic History of the Maritime Provinces*. Ottawa, 1939. Accessed at https://archive.org.

Shaw, Beatrice M. Hay. "The Vanishing Folklore of Nova Scotia." *Dalhousie Review* 3 issue 3 (1923): 342-49.

About the Author

JUDY ROY grew up in Worcester, Massachusetts, the eldest child of Anne Marie (Nicholson) and Paul Kiritsy. She studied chemistry at St. Francis Xavier University in Antigonish, Nova Scotia, and earned a Ph.D. in Pharmacology at the University of Kentucky in Lexington. She has co-authored scientific research papers on pain and analgesia in neuropharmacology. In recent years, her interests have shifted to genealogy and family history. Mother of two and grandmother of five, she lives with her husband Mark in Browns Summit, North Carolina.

www.ingramcontent.com/pod-product-compliance
Lightning Source LLC
Chambersburg PA
CBHW060908120626
46553CB00001B/252